Destiny is a buzzword of the modern church. However, realizing destiny in one's life is the result of making the right decisions at critical junctures in life. Making right decisions is based upon following the right principles, so fulfillment of destiny results from knowing the principles that will help you make the right choices. In her book *God's Order*, Patti Hedgepath Lusk has rendered a service to all who are pursuing their destiny by outlining many life-altering principles in a way that is easily understood and easily applied.

—Dr. Ronald Carpenter, Sr.
Presiding Bishop
International Pentecostal Holiness Church

A refreshing guidebook to the rediscovery of God's order. Patti Hedgepath Lusk charts the course for the successful navigation of the maze of twenty-first century living. A must-read for all who desire to understand God's plan for our life and our world.

—Dr. John R. Benson
Pastor Emeritus
Shady Grove Baptist Church

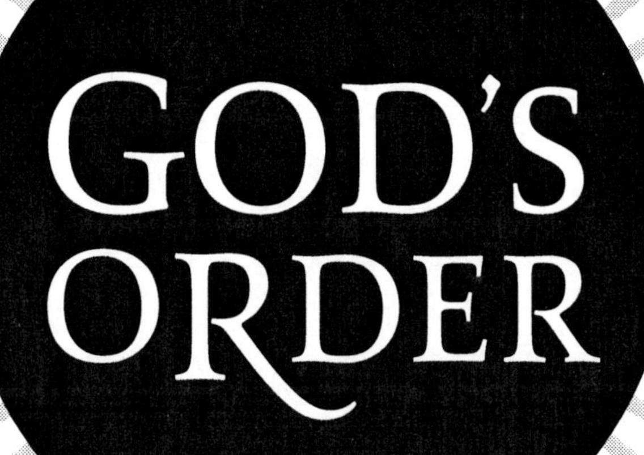

GOD'S
ORDER

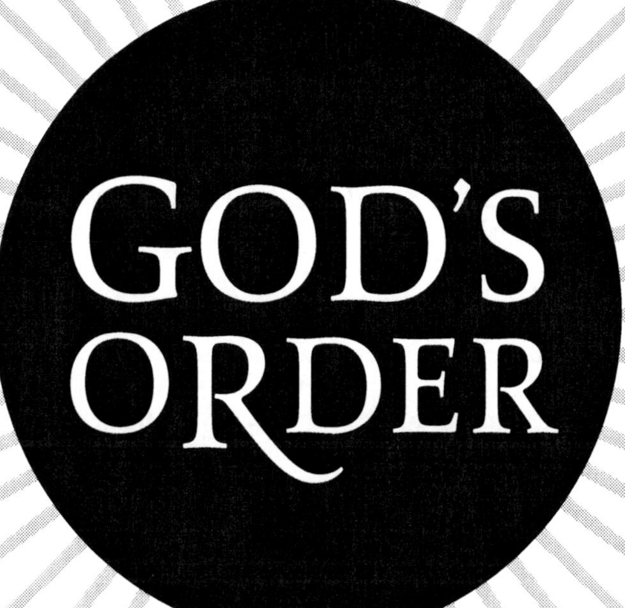

GOD'S ORDER

PATTI HEDGEPATH LUSK

God's Order by Patti Hedgepath Lusk
Published by Creation House
A Strang Company
600 Rinehart Road
Lake Mary, Florida 32746
www.strangbookgroup.com

Unless otherwise noted, all Scripture quotations are from the King James Version of the Bible.

Scripture quotations marked AMP are from the Amplified Bible. Old Testament copyright © 1965, 1987 by the Zondervan Corporation. The Amplified New Testament copyright © 1954, 1958, 1987 by the Lockman Foundation. Used by permission.

English definitions are taken from *Webster's New World Dictionary.*

Hebrew definitions are taken from *Strong's Exhaustive Concordance of the Bible* (Peabody, MA: Hendrickson Publishers, 2009).

Greek definitions are taken from *Strong's Exhaustive Concordance of the Bible* (Peabody, MA: Hendrickson Publishers, 2009) and *Vine's Expository Dictionary of New Testament Words* (Nashville, TN: Royal Publishers, Inc., nd).

Design Director: Bill Johnson

Cover design by Justin Evans

Library of Congress Control Number: 2010926536
International Standard Book Number: 978-1-61638-171-4

First Edition

10 11 12 13 14 — 9 8 7 6 5 4 3 2 1
Printed in the United States of America

Contents

Preface

MOST CHRISTIAN BOOKS and messages are written under the supposition that the reader understands the order of God. In these days that is often not the case. People need to be taught the basics of the Christian life. We need foundational teaching and instruction before we can understand the deeper things of God.

The instructions on the pages of this book are about the order of the world and the people in it as designed by God in the beginning. It is not to condemn those who choose not to live according to God's order. Rather, it is a guide for those who want to know the truth so they can follow it.

This book is also to serve as a reminder to a generation in a world where Christian principles are considered obsolete. Even the Christian population seems to have lost its mooring and is experiencing confusion on Christian teachings. The whole world is looking for peace, and, ironically, the path to peace is spelled out clearly and systematically in a book many reject—the Bible. If one person here and another there will be enlightened, all the effort will be worthwhile. There is nothing new in the pages you have before you. But, we need to be reminded, lest we forget the Lord our God and a generation rises up that does not know the Lord Jehovah nor the sacrifice of His Son Jesus nor the working of His Spirit among men.

Let truth arise in the heart of everyone who reads these words, and let God be glorified in their lives.

Introduction

IF WE WANT to understand God's commandments, we need to understand His order from the beginning.

Many may say, "Why go back to the creation?" The answer is simple. That is where our history began. God had no beginning, nor does He have an end; but mankind does have a beginning. If we don't understand our beginnings and the order of God in creation, marriage, laws (made necessary because of the fall of mankind), and our ultimate redemption, the teachings of Jesus will not be clear to us. When we can comprehend the primary order of God at Creation and before the Fall, we can better understand the need for law, sacrifices, and redemption.

The teachings of Jesus and the mission of Jesus are based on the old covenant and God's first dealings with mankind. Jesus said He didn't come to do away with the Law but to fulfill it. If we do not believe God is Creator, we do not believe in Jesus. If we do not believe the commandments of God, we do not believe the commandments of Jesus. If we do not believe the laws of marriage as set forth in the beginning, then we do not believe the laws of marriage as set forth by Jesus. If we believe God's Word, we need to understand why. There is a thread of order that runs all the way through the Scriptures.

First Peter 3:15 tells us to "be ready always to give an answer to every man that asketh you a reason of the hope that is in you with meekness and fear." We need to know why we believe what we believe, and the answer begins at the beginning. These teachings used to be common knowledge taught in our churches, but they are often neglected today as they have become controversial in a liberal world. It is easier to teach doctrines that are more "acceptable." The pattern of the world system has crept into our churches, and many churches no longer uphold pure Christian doctrine as found in God's Word.

Without the foundational principles of God, we cannot stand. Every secure structure has a sturdy, trustworthy foundation. If the base of the building is unsure, the integrity of the whole building is at risk. If our belief in God is not sturdy and trustworthy, then our whole lives are in danger of toppling over at any time. We must dig deep, down to the Rock, to make sure our foundation is stable. Then we can begin to build something lasting and worthwhile in this world and the world to come.

If our beliefs about God change from day to day or we spend our lives going through phases about what we believe and do not believe, we are double minded. James 1:8 warns us, "A double minded man is unstable in all his ways." If we vacillate in our opinion of who God is and His purposes, we will be inconstant in our whole course of life. Our actions will be sporadic and purposeless. We may be busy, yet accomplish little. We will be like a tall building teetering and tottering because of a weak foundation. (Other passages that involve the folly of double lives are James 3:8–18, 2 Corinthians 6:14–18, Matthew 6:24, and Ephesians 4:21–32.) God is consistently the same.

The Lord has something much better for us. He wants us to *know* Him. He wants us to build on a foundation that is sure and has purpose. "Jesus Christ the same yesterday, and to day, and for ever" (Heb. 13:8). We can count on that truth.

Jesus told us how to have the right foundation in Luke 6:46–49. That involves obeying His teachings, which are based on the order of God from the beginning of time.

> And why call ye me, Lord, Lord, and do not the things which I say? Whosoever cometh to me, and heareth my sayings, and doeth them, I will shew you to whom he is like: He is like a man which built an house, and digged deep, and laid the foundation on a rock: and when the flood arose, the stream beat vehemently upon that house, and could not shake it: for it was founded upon a rock. But he that heareth, and doeth not, is like a man that without a foundation built an house upon the earth; against which the stream did beat vehemently, and immediately it fell; and the ruin of that house was great.

If we do not believe the very basics of God's order, we have a shaky foundation at best. If our foundation is questionable, anything we try to build on it will eventually crumble, for without knowledge of the primary teachings and commandments of God, we will accept false doctrine as well as truth. We don't have to flounder in our faith. We can stand strong and firm.

Although we cannot understand all the details of God's character and His deeds, there are so many things He does want us to know and understand. We can understand the basic facts of God's order. We then choose to believe or disbelieve. Believing is not just a mental task; it is placing our whole self on the foundation of God—everything we do and say. If we truly believe, we will allow God to change our mind-set and lifestyle to agree with His order. If we want our lives set in God's order, we will cooperate with the changes He speaks to us through study of His Word and time in His presence.

God has wonderfully supplied us with a touchstone with which to compare all our ideas and all our programs. It is His Word. Do we question a certain tradition or new fad in the churches? We can go directly to the Bible for the answer; and, with the help of the Holy Spirit, we can understand what is right and true.

What is God's order? Order is a state in which every part is where it should be functioning properly. It works according to a certain system, which is a set of things brought together to form a whole, such as the solar system. It implies a way of doing something in an orderly manner. First Corinthians 14:33, in speaking of God's order in the church, reveals this about God: "For God is not the author of confusion, but of peace, as in all churches of the saints." *Peace* simply means "to be set at one with God." He is a God of order—in creation, in the institution of marriage, in commandments and covenant, in judgment, in redemption, in the institution of the church, and in His kingdom, the redemption of all things. God's order runs consistently throughout time and beyond time.

Before we can believe in God's order, we must believe that God is. That is an imperative and necessary first step. We can learn about God through the Holy Scriptures and personally from His Spirit when we are born again. Too many people are not totally convinced that God is who the Bible says He is and has the power and authority that scriptures declare Him to own. We cannot choose to believe part of the Holy Scriptures and not the other. If part of it is false, how do we know we can rely on Christ for salvation? Are we intellectual enough to decipher which parts to believe and which to deny or reject? If we try to build our knowledge and experience with the Lord while our belief (total reliance on Him) is unsettled, we will experience frustration and have disaster looming over us as we watch our edifice sway, shake, and fall. Our faith is unable to grow because we have lost sight of our foundation—God's order. First, we must believe God is who He says He is in the Bible. That is the most basic foundation.

chapter one

God Is

IN THE BEGINNING God...." (Gen. 1:1). Before we explore what God *did* in the beginning, let's start with the first layer. Let's explore who God was, is, and is to come.

He has many names, but each one simply explains a portion of His character in pictures and words we can understand. The following list is by no means complete but will, hopefully, renew our wonder and awe at the almighty God. They show us who He is. Of course, we cannot fully understand God, for He is too great. "For My thoughts are not your thoughts, neither are your ways my ways, saith the LORD. For as the heavens are higher than the earth, so are my ways higher than your ways, and my thoughts than your thoughts" (Isa. 55:8–9). A knowledge of who God is will help us trust Him for all the things we cannot understand. There is much He desires to reveal to us and will reveal to those who seek after the truth of God. Those who sincerely want to know Him can know Him and have spiritual blessings of wisdom and discernment. He reveals much of Himself through His Word and by His Spirit. (See 1 Corinthians 2:9–16.)

Seek ye the LORD while he may be found, call ye upon him while he is near.

—ISAIAH 55:6

But without faith it is impossible to please him: for he that cometh to God must believe that he is, and that he is a rewarder of them that diligently seek him.

—HEBREWS 11:6

Ask, and it shall be given you; seek, and ye shall find; knock, and it shall be opened unto you: For every one that asketh receiveth; and he that seeketh findeth; and to him that knocketh it shall be opened. Or what man is there of you, whom if his son ask bread, will he give him a stone? Or if he ask a fish, will he give him a serpent? If ye then, being evil, know how to give good gifts unto your children, how much more shall your Father which is in heaven give good things to them that ask him?

—MATTHEW 7:7–11

Too often we take these scriptures as grounds to ask God for *things* instead of to know Him. We need the Lord's Spirit and His Word (the guide and roadmap) to take us deep into the territory of God's nature. (See 1 Corinthians 1:1–16 and 2 Timothy 3:13–17.) If you have a map but don't understand how to read it, you need a guide to go along and explain it to you. God's Spirit will enlighten us to the depth of His Word.

The names of God as listed in the Bible give us a clear picture of His character, which reveals His desire for us to know Him. The word *name* means "character and authority." It is all that the name implies—glory, honor, majesty, authority, and every other part of His character. Here is a list of some of His names.

Lord God

Genesis 2:4: "These are the generations of the heavens and of the earth when they were created, in the day that the LORD God made the earth and the heavens." (See also Genesis 15:2, 8.) The Lord is the One who is self-existent, who is supreme in authority, and who controls all things. God is the supreme divinity. He exceeds all others in rank, power, quality, accomplishments, honor, and majesty. (Read that list again, very slowly.) There is only one true God, and He is in control of everything. He is the final word. "Hear, O Israel: The LORD our God is one LORD" (Deut. 6:4).

Almighty God

Genesis 17:1: "And when Abram was ninety years old and nine, the LORD appeared to Abram, and said unto him, I am the Almighty God; walk before me, and be thou perfect." This name for God comes from the Hebrew *El Shaddai,* meaning "the all-sufficient One" or "the all-powerful One" (omnipotent). There is nothing that can penetrate through His power and might. Not only does He possess the ability, but the right or authority to act. "Ah Lord GOD! behold, thou hast made the heaven and the earth by thy great power and stretched out arm, and there is nothing too hard for thee" (Jer. 32:17). "For with God nothing shall be impossible" (Luke 1:37). There is no problem God cannot solve, no situation He cannot change, no disease He cannot heal, no mountain He cannot move. He has proven it in the past, and He is still all-powerful!

I AM

Exodus 3:14: "And God said unto Moses, I AM THAT I AM: and he said, Thus shalt thou say unto the children of Israel, I AM hath sent me unto you." I AM is the very essence of God, His basic nature. He *is*. He *is* love. He *is* peace. He *is*! He exists, and this title is always used emphatically. This is the ultimate question we must ask ourselves before we can believe in any other Bible doctrine: Do we believe God is?

Jehovah

Exodus 6:3: "And I appeared unto Abraham, unto Isaac, and unto Jacob, by the name of God Almighty, but by my name JEHOVAH was I not known to them." *Jehovah* is the same as *Lord*—the One who is self-existent (uncreated, but has always been and always will be) and who has supreme authority and control. This is Jehovah. The name "God Almighty" showed His power and authority (what He can do), but "Jehovah" and "Lord God" show more of His character (who He is). We know the power and authority the president of the United States has; but few know him personally, so few know his real nature and character—his heart. God wields His power from His heart, or character.

Psalm 103:7 says that God "made known his ways unto Moses, his acts unto the children of Israel." The Israelites wanted God to speak to Moses and then let Moses speak to them. They were afraid of His presence, so they only saw what God did; they didn't get to know Him personally. We can get to know God on a personal level and be familiar with His characteristics that cause Him to do what He does and say what He says. If you are close to someone for a long time, you can pretty well know how they will respond to certain circumstances and what they expect because you have learned their character and ways firsthand. God wants to reveal Himself to us and will *when we draw close to Him.*

Most High God

Genesis 14:18–22: "And Melchizedek king of Salem brought forth bread and wine: and he was the priest of the most high God. And he blessed him, and said, Blessed be Abram of the most high God, possessor of heaven and earth: And blessed be the most high God, which hath delivered thine enemies into thy hand." The most high God is the One who is lifted above all, the Lord God. There is no other who He answers to or is subject to. He is preeminent. There is an adage that says, "The buck stops here." That refers to God.

Everlasting God

Genesis 21:33: "And Abraham planted a grove in Beersheba, and called there on the name of the Lord, the everlasting God." God is not here today and gone tomorrow. He is *from* everlasting *to* everlasting. (See Psalms 41:13, 90:2, 103:17, and 106:48.) We can understand that concept more clearly when we realize God is the *eternal* God. Deuteronomy 33:27 tells us, "The eternal God is thy refuge, and underneath are the everlasting arms." *Eternal* means "forever in both directions." He is eternal going into the past and into the future. That is the same as *from* everlasting *to* everlasting.

Like a circle, with God there is no beginning or ending, and He is not limited by time. The eternal God has already been in our future. He was before time began and will be when time is no more. God always has been and always will be. "I am Alpha and Omega, the beginning and the ending, saith the Lord, which is, and which was, and which is to come, the Almighty" (Rev. 1:8). *Alpha* and *omega* are the first and last letters of the Greek alphabet. He is the First and the Last and everything in between. This emphasizes the continuity of God. He has no creator but is the Creator of all things. Can I understand it? No. Do I believe it? Yes, because all I know and have experienced of God lets me know He is true.

Jealous God

Exodus 34:14: "For thou shalt worship no other god: for the Lord, whose name is Jealous, is a jealous God."

There is only one God who is truly God. He is zealous in rewarding those who believe Him and seek Him, as we read in Hebrews 11:6. He is zealous in purging those who serve false gods. Nor will He tolerate those who try to worship Him *and* other gods. He will not tolerate lip service from a heart that is far from Him. Our God is jealous over us. He desires us to have the very best, and He provides it. He hates every false way because it leads us to destruction, and He is jealous for our redemption and blessing.

Living God

Joshua 3:10: "And Joshua said, Hereby ye shall know that the living God is among you, and that he will without fail drive out from before you the Canaanites, and the Hittites, and the Hivites, and the Perizzites, and the Girgashites, and the Amorites, and the Jebusites." This God is not an idol of wood, stone, or metal. Nor is He a sentimental god we make up in our minds. He is alive and in charge. He is alive enough to drive out the enemies because He is the Lord of Hosts. God is the God of a mighty host—the God of Heaven's armies. *Host* usually means "a large number of people prepared and ready for war." "Therefore saith the Lord, the Lord of hosts, the mighty One of Israel, Ah, I will ease me of mine adversaries, and avenge me of mine enemies" (Isa. 1:24). God's wrath is poured out upon evil, and He will crush it completely. God hates evil because it destroys what is good. Sin separates us from Him and will destroy us. Certainly He has a host of angels that do His bidding, as well as a host of those who serve Him in the earth. We don't fight against flesh and blood but against wicked spirits. (See Ephesians 6:12.)

> Lift up your heads, O ye gates; and be ye lift up, ye everlasting doors; and the King of glory shall come in. Who is this King of glory? The LORD strong and mighty, the LORD mighty in battle. Lift up your heads, O ye gates; even lift them up, ye everlasting doors; and the King of glory shall come in. Who is this King of glory? The LORD of hosts, he is the King of glory. Selah.
>
> —PSALM 24:7–10

Holy One

Isaiah 43:15: "I am the LORD, your Holy One, the creator of Israel, your King." God is holy. He is sacred, pure, sinless, perfect, and complete. There is no sin or darkness in God. "But as he which hath called you is holy, so be ye holy in all manner of conversation [character]; Because it is written, Be ye holy; for I am holy" (1 Pet. 1:15–16). He invites us to be holy through His holiness and righteous through His righteousness. He is such pure light, that He casts no shadow. (See James 1:17.) There is nothing even slightly tainted in Him.

King

First Timothy 1:17: "Now unto the King eternal, immortal, invisible, the only wise God, be honour and glory for ever and ever. Amen." God as King is the foundation of power that holds everything together—the universe and all it contains. This verse describes the King as eternal, immortal (not subject to death), invisible (not seen with the natural eye but more real than we are), and the *only* wise God. Other gods are merely manmade idols that "have mouths, but they speak not; eyes have they, but they see not; They have ears, but they hear not; neither is there any breath in their mouths. They that make them are like unto them: so is every one that trusteth in them" (Ps. 135:16–18). His wisdom is clear, transparent. He will make His truth clear to those who know Him and seek after Him. Because of these characteristics, He is worthy to receive honor and glory forever.

Only Potentate

First Timothy 6:15: "Which in his times he shall shew, who is the blessed and only Potentate, the King of kings and Lord of lords." There is only one ruler who is able to make all things possible. All others merely receive what power God chooses to give them. "For promotion cometh neither from the east, nor from the west, nor from the south. But God is the judge: he putteth down one, and setteth up another" (Ps. 75:6–7). There is not another who comes close. He is the only such ruler. He is the King above all other kings and the Lord above all other lords. God, and God alone, determines which kings or lesser rulers will rule and for how long. There is no question that this God *is*.

There are various ways God has revealed Himself to

His people. The Bible is full of examples of how God's characteristics directly affect His people. What we believe about God will not change who He is but can change who we are. God is who He is regardless of what we do and who we are. His characteristics remain the same, yet He wants to fellowship with us and to reveal Himself to us. If we seek Him, He will show Himself to us at various times of our lives, as the following names indicate.

Jehovah-jireh—The Lord Our Provider

Genesis 22:13–14: "And Abraham lifted up his eyes, and looked, and behold behind him a ram caught in a thicket by his horns: and Abraham went and took the ram, and offered him up for a burnt offering in the stead of his son. And Abraham called the name of that place Jehovah-jireh: as it is said to this day, In the mount of the LORD it shall be seen."

Jehovah has been revealed over and over in the life of His people as the provider of our needs. Read in the Old Testament of God providing the ram for Abraham to offer up rather than his son, of manna falling from Heaven to feed His people, of the mouths of the lions being stopped for Daniel, of Esther and her people being protected from harm, and of many more instances where God revealed Himself as Jehovah-jireh. This is personal involvement in the lives of His people down through time. He is still the provider of those who rely on Him and trust His leadership enough to follow.

Jehovah-nissi—The Lord Our Banner

Exodus 17:15–16: "And Moses built an altar, and called the name of it Jehovah-nissi: for he said, Because the LORD hath sworn that the LORD will have war with Amalek from generation to generation." Whatever battle we face, if we will rest in Jehovah-nissi, He will go before us as our Banner. When our troops fight under the flag or banner of the United States of America, everyone knows by whose authority and power they fight. When we face battles in our lives, if we are under the authority of Jesus Christ, He is our Banner; the enemy knows the power and authority of Jesus Christ goes before us. We go in the name (character and authority) of Jesus, the Anointed One, the Lord our Banner.

Jehovah-shalom—The Lord Our Peace

Judges 6:23–24: When the angel of the Lord appeared to Gideon to call him into service for the Lord, Gideon was afraid. "And the LORD said unto him, Peace be unto thee; fear not: thou shalt not die. Then Gideon built an altar there unto the LORD, and called it Jehovah-shalom." The Lord is peace. His peace is not like the world's peace, which only entails the absence of war or getting along with those around you. His peace means we are set at one with Him again. We are not in opposition to Him but are in fellowship with Him because the sin that separated us has been forgiven and removed completely by the blood of Jesus Christ.

"And let the peace of God rule in your hearts, to the

which also ye are called in one body; and be ye thankful" (Col. 3:15). This is how individualized our relationship is with God. When we realize our peace is broken, we know we have stepped away from His presence. We can correct our error and get back on the right path.

"Be careful [anxious] for nothing; but in every thing by prayer and supplication with thanksgiving let your requests be made known unto God. And the peace of God, which passeth all understanding, shall keep your hearts and minds, through Christ Jesus" (Phil. 4:6–7). Being at one with Jesus will give us knowledge and wisdom beyond human understanding. Once again, He reveals Himself through this peace that goes beyond human intellect. He gives us a dimension in our lives that Jesus called "life more abundant" (John 10:10). These aspects of God's character He chooses to reveal to us on a personal level. But we must be willing and come on His terms, His order.

Jehovah-raah—The Lord My Shepherd

Psalm 23:1: "The LORD is my shepherd; I shall not want." Psalm 23 gives the details of how the Lord cares for and protects us. All we need to do is follow His leading and trust Him to take care of everything else. When we need the green pastures, He knows and will lead us there. When we need the refreshment of still waters, He will show us the best place. Even in times of heartache and trial, this Lord, this Shepherd of our souls, is with us to see that we have safe passage. Do you know Him *personally* as the Shepherd?

Jehovah-tsidkenu—The Lord Our Righteousness

Jeremiah 23:6: "In his [Jesus'] days Judah shall be saved, and Israel shall dwell safely: and this is his name whereby he shall be called, THE LORD OUR RIGHTEOUSNESS." We cannot make ourselves righteous, but He is completely righteous. We cannot attain righteousness (right standing with God) any other way except through faith in Jesus Christ. Ephesians 4:24 tells us to "put on the new man, which after God is created in righteousness and true holiness." Although we cannot make ourselves righteous, we can be born of the Spirit of God and be made righteous and holy by His Spirit alive within us. We become new creatures in Christ, our Righteousness. (See 2 Corinthians 5:17.)

Jehovah-shammah—The Lord Is Present

Second Corinthians 6:16: "And what agreement hath the temple of God with idols? for ye are the temple of the living God; as God hath said, I will dwell in them, and walk in them; and I will be their God, and they shall be my people." How close is the relationship between God and His people? He dwells *in* us. Our bodies have become the temple of the living God. Just as He was present with Israel under the old covenant in the ark of the covenant in the tabernacle and later the temple, He is present within us. He is near. The prophet Ezekiel told of the coming destruction of Jerusalem and the temple because of the sin of God's people. He foretold the dispersal of his people into heathen lands. But in Ezekiel 11:16, God says,

"Although I have cast them far off among the heathen, and although I have scattered them among the countries, yet will I be to them as a little sanctuary in the countries where they shall come." God was punishing them, but He did not forsake them. He is present with us even in times of trial and correction.

Jehovah-mekaddishkem—The Lord Our Sanctifier

Leviticus 20:26: "And ye shall be holy unto me: for I the LORD am holy, and have severed you from other people, that ye should be mine." Those who are truly born again are to be separated *from* sin and *unto* the Lord. "What? know ye not that your body is the temple of the Holy Ghost which is in you, which ye have of God, and ye are not your own? For ye are bought with a price: therefore glorify God in your body, and in your spirit, which are God's" (1 Cor. 6:19–20). The price of our redemption was great. The cost was the blood of the Son of God. When we separate ourselves from the practices of the world and to the principles of God's Word, we receive many blessings, the most prominent being rescued from sin and its consequences. We have a relationship with the Lord that is impossible without being cleansed from sin. We also have great responsibilities, for we are no longer our own, but belong to the Lord. We have been set apart for His glory and work.

Jesus of Nazareth, the Christ—Anointed One

Hebrews 1:1–3: "God, who at sundry times and in divers manners spake in time past unto the fathers by the prophets, Hath in these last days spoken unto us by his Son, whom he hath appointed heir of all things, by whom also he made the worlds; Who being the brightness of his glory, and the express image [exact copy] of his person, and upholding all things by the word of his power, when he had by himself purged our sins, sat down on the right hand of the Majesty on high." The clearest revelation of God was through His Son, Jesus. They are one. John 1 declares that Jesus was there at Creation and nothing was made without Him. He is God who took on human flesh in order to save us. He lived among men, and we have a written account of His life. This account gives us a glimpse at the character of God, the purpose of God, the wisdom of God, the power of God, and the love of God. Someone once said that Jesus put a face on God for us. "And the Word was made flesh, and dwelt among us, (and we beheld his glory, the glory as of the only begotten of the Father,) full of grace and truth" (John 1:14).

These are just a few of the ways God reveals Himself to His people, but they are enough to give us insight into the great price God paid to make it possible for us to draw close to Him and get to know Him.

There are several passages in the Scriptures that give us a glimpse of the glory of the throne room where God dwells. Among them is Revelation 4:2–5:

> And immediately I was in the spirit: and, behold,
> a throne was set in heaven, and one sat on the
> throne. And he that sat was to look upon like

a jasper and a sardine stone: and there was a rainbow round about the throne, in sight like unto an emerald. And round about the throne were four and twenty seats: and upon the seats I saw four and twenty elders sitting, clothed in white raiment; and they had on their heads crowns of gold. And out of the throne proceeded lightnings and thunderings and voices: and there were seven lamps of fire burning before the throne, which are the seven Spirits of God.

This is an awesome description that is more wonderful than my mind can imagine. We have a powerful, majestic God. Other passages that give like descriptions are found in Ezekiel 1:26–28, Revelation 1:10–18, and Daniel 7:9–10.

Now, is this the God we know? Do we have the right kind of reverence for this awesome God? Are we persuaded within our hearts that we believe God is all that He says He is in His Word? This information is foundational to everything else in our world. If we indeed believe Him to be who the Bible says He is, our lives will show it. The word *believe* means more than mental assent. The word *believe* means to be so confident of who Jesus is that we trust Him completely and rely on Him in every aspect of our lives. It is not just credence to a doctrine. If we truly have confidence in someone and trust his or her word, we will act upon it. The word of some people I take with a grain of salt, because either they have proven to be untrustworthy or I don't know them well enough to know if they are. But I will believe and act on the words of those whom I have learned I can trust. I have found God to be faithful in all His dealings with me. I have found His Word to be true.

When we renew our vision of who God really is and accept Him as who He is, we can go on to the order He has set up.

chapter 2

Creation

OUR WORLD IS in chaos. There is worldwide unrest, violence, distrust, and turmoil. Everyone is searching for a new order that will end the upheaval and bring peace and unity. But there is no manmade, new order that can accomplish such a needed objective. As a matter of fact, the time is coming when it seems such a plan will be implemented, but it will fail miserably after three and one-half years of false peace. (See Daniel 9:27.)

Genuine peace can only be based on truth, honor, and integrity. That is God's order. His order has been established from the beginning. Rather than trying to find and establish a new order, we need to practice God's order established from the beginning and going on through eternity.

This world was created with perfect balance among the plants, animals, people, and their Creator. We do not experience the peace and harmony of His order because most people do not walk in His order. When sin entered the picture, it disrupted the perfection God created and caused us to live outside His perfect order. It will not always be that way, and it was not that way in the beginning. "In the beginning God created the heaven and the earth" (Gen. 1:1).

Although God has always been and always will be, we live in an interval called time. It is the period between eternity past and eternity future. Time involves "every moment that has ever been and every moment that ever will be."

Some scholars believe time was created when the earth was created. That may or may not be accurate, but the fact remains that we are limited by time. If we ask ourselves, In the beginning of what? "time" seems the obvious answer.

The origin, or the starting point, of Heaven and Earth is simple. God created them. Then He set about putting everything into order. There is a set arrangement of things in our universe because God had an orderly plan that He spoke into existence. If one small change occurred in the tilt of the earth or the revolutionary paths of the planets, the whole solar system could be destroyed.

"And the earth was without form, and void; and darkness was upon the face of the deep. And the Spirit of God moved upon the face of the waters. And God said, Let there be light: and there was light" (Gen. 1:2 3). God called the earth out of chaos into order, out of darkness to light. His Word was powerful enough to command the obedience of every element.

> In the beginning was the Word, and the Word
> was with God, and the Word was God. The same

was in the beginning with God. All things were made by him; and without him was not any thing made that was made. In him was life; and the life was the light of men.

—JOHN 1:1–4

Jesus, the Word, was there in the beginning. He did not just suddenly appear as a tiny baby in Bethlehem. He always has been and is the revelation of God. Nothing was made without Him.

Darkness covered the earth, so God spoke light into existence. He put a division between light and darkness. The first day, God created night and day. (See Genesis 1:4–5.) Before that time, there was darkness, but God is light and He shed light on the earth.

The second day God divided the waters from the waters with the firmament between them. God called the firmament heaven. (See Genesis 1:6–8.) The firmament is the expanse of the sky as we see it above us. There were now waters above the heavens and waters beneath.

On day three God gathered the waters under the heaven into one place and caused the dry land to appear. "And God called the dry land Earth; and the gathering together of the waters called he Seas: and God saw that it was good" (Gen. 1:10). Rather than a world covered entirely with water, God caused the water to come together in seas and allow dry land to appear in various places.

Also, in the third day God created plants and trees to grow on the earth. He created them to reproduce after their own kind. The seed was in them to produce more grass or trees. There is incredible detail included in the reproduction of plants. It could not and did not happen by chance. God's order is detailed. His designs are intricate. Not being very scientifically minded, I cannot describe just how all this comes about, but it does. I have heard it explained in lectures, and it baffled my mind. Yet, we watch it take place routinely in our lives. Apple trees produce apples, which contain seeds to produce more apple trees, which in turn produce apples with seeds…And we could go on endlessly. The pattern God spoke into existence for plants goes on still today. They continue to function within the system God commanded in the beginning. The wonder of God's creation is amazing. We take it for granted because we were born into this world and grew up with these natural happenings around us every day. But every creation testifies of a Creator.

Next, God created the sun, moon, and stars and placed them in the firmament of the heaven. These lights were to divide the day from the night. They were also put there for signs and seasons, days, and years and to give light to the earth. God balanced everything perfectly to carry out His plan. God knows every star by name. "He telleth the number of the stars; he calleth them all by their names. Great is our Lord, and of great power: his understanding is infinite" (Ps. 147:4–5, see also Isa. 40:21–26). He knows every detail. Nothing escapes His notice. "And the evening and the morning were the fourth day" (Gen. 1:19).

On day five God created birds of all descriptions and the

water animals, all after their kind or species. A species is a distinct type of plant or animal that has specific characteristics distinguishing it. In other words, birds did not turn into water creatures or water creatures into birds. Eagles reproduced eagles. Whales reproduced whales. Although dogs have different varieties, they stay within their species or kind. This is God's order in creation. Also, in the plant kingdom each plant reproduced within its own species. Reproduction of plants and animals continues on today just as God set it in motion in the beginning. "And God blessed them, saying, Be fruitful, and multiply, and fill the waters in the seas, and let fowl multiply in the earth" (Gen. 1:22).

The sixth day was the last of the Creation and setting up of God's order in the natural things of this earth. On this day God made every land animal after its kind. Again, His order prevailed in reproducing their own species. But God wasn't through once He created the beasts.

> And God said, Let us make man in our image, after our likeness: and let them have dominion over the fish of the sea, and over the fowl of the air, and over the cattle, and over all the earth, and over every creeping thing that creepeth upon the earth. So God created man in his own image, and in the image of God created he him; male and female created he them. And God blessed them, and God said unto them, Be fruitful, and multiply, and replenish the earth, and subdue it: and have dominion over the fish of the sea, and

over the fowl of the air, and over every living thing that moveth upon the earth.

—Genesis 1:26–28

In Genesis 2 we have more of the details of the creation of man and woman. Man was molded from the dust of the ground, and the Lord God "breathed into his nostrils the breath of life; and man became a living soul" (Gen. 2:7). God blew of His Spirit into the man, and that divine inspiration kindled a distinct depth of life and intellect into the body of the first man, Adam. He did not breathe that dimension of life into the animals. Mankind has a unique reasoning ability.

After causing a deep sleep to fall upon Adam, God took one of Adam's ribs and made a woman from it. No animal could be found as a helper that was suitable or appropriate for him. God specially made an assistant for Adam. God Himself had breathed into him the breath of life. Adam was to have dominion over all the animals, not be on the same level with them. Mankind was given a higher capacity of intellect, reasoning, and spirit.

God's order found in Genesis 1:26–28 specifies that man is superior to animals and plants and is to take dominion over them. We are not equal. The living soul of man separates him from the animals. Humans are to bear rule over animals.

Psalm 8:3–9 upholds God's order of animals being ruled by mankind:

When I consider thy heavens, the work of thy fingers, the moon and the stars, which thou hast ordained; What is man, that thou art mindful of him? and the son of man, that thou visitest him? For thou hast made him a little lower than the angels, and hast crowned him with glory and honour. Thou madest him to have dominion over the works of thy hands; thou hast put all things under his feet: All sheep and oxen, yea, and the beasts of the field; The fowl of the air, and the fish of the sea, and whatsoever passeth through the paths of the seas. O LORD our Lord, how excellent is thy name in all the earth!

It is clear that animals are not given the same prominence as humanity, but this does not mean that animals are to be evilly treated. We are still the keepers of God's creation. Proverbs 12:10 speaks of treating animals kindly: "A righteous man regardeth the life of his beast: but the tender mercies of the wicked are cruel." Jesus spoke of the heavenly Father's care of the birds in Matthew 6:26: "Behold the fowls of the air: for they sow not, neither do they reap, nor gather into barns; yet your heavenly Father feedeth them, Are ye not much better than they?" There is a distinction of dominance in humanity, although God cares for all His creation. Humankind has been placed in a position of rulership over all other creatures, which not only denotes honor but responsibility. We are the keepers or guards of God's creation and should never mistreat any of it. "And God saw every thing that he had made, and, behold, it was very good" (Gen. 1:31).

God brought His creation to perfection and rested on the seventh day, or completed His work. His order was set, and nature continues to produce and reproduce. Generations come and generations go. None of this just happened; the Creator made it all and blessed it. If something is created, there must be a Creator.

Down through time God has proven many times His power as master of His creation. He has done marvelous things for His people and for His glory in the past (and even now). He caused the sun to stand still on one occasion, caused a donkey to speak, caused the Jordan River to stop flowing, and parted the Red Sea. Jesus showed His authority over nature when He calmed the storm and sea, raised the dead, healed bodies, fed thousands with one lunch, walked on the water, and showed His mastery over every other spirit when He cast out demons. He is master of everything.

God did not create the world and all in it just to leave it alone. He is active in the life of every person and all of His creation. His order is established under His dominion.

chapter 3

Marriage

WHEN GOD CREATED man and woman, He instituted marriage. Marriage is the union of one man and one woman as planned by God. Anything outside of that is outside of God's order.

> And Adam gave names to all cattle, and to the fowl of the air, and to every beast of the field; but for Adam there was not found an help meet for him. And the LORD God caused a deep sleep to fall upon Adam, and he slept: and he took one of his ribs, and closed up the flesh instead thereof; And the rib, which the Lord God had taken from man, made he a woman, and brought her unto the man.
>
> —GENESIS 2:20–22

After finding no match for Adam among His creation, God made a woman from the man in whom He had breathed the breath of life. When the work was complete, God presented Adam with His newest creation. She was a suitable partner, as the Scriptures tell us in Genesis 2:23–24:

> And Adam said, This is now bone of my bones, and flesh of my flesh: she shall be called Woman,

> because she was taken out of Man. Therefore shall a man leave his father and his mother, and shall cleave unto his wife: and they shall be one flesh.

This is the bedrock on which to base every marriage. One man, one woman, joined together for life, forsaking all others.

Ephesians 5 gives us God's pattern of what marriage is supposed to be. To accomplish this type of relationship, it takes both parties doing their part. The wives are instructed to "submit yourselves unto your own husbands, as unto the Lord. For the husband is the head of the wife, even as Christ is the head of the church: and he is the saviour of the body" (Eph. 5:22–23). This could be interpreted as a set-up for anarchy and total domination, but God speaks to the husbands, too. He has an order here. God has chosen the man as the leader of the home but not the dictator. Every good leader considers those who follow them more than they consider their own gain.

> But I would have you know, that the head of every man is Christ; and the head of the woman is the man; and the head of Christ is God.... Neither was the man created for the woman; but the woman for the man.... Nevertheless neither is the man without the woman, neither the woman without the man, in the Lord. For as the woman is of the man, even so is the man also by the woman; but all things of God.
>
> —1 CORINTHIANS 11:3, 9, 11–12

The husband is the authority of the home and gives it direction. The wife is to come alongside and be the help he needs. They are to complete one another.

If order is to be maintained, a leader is needed, a leader with authority and the respect of those under him. If a troop of soldiers tries to march in step without a leader calling out the cadence, it is impossible to stay in order. If the leader calls the step but no one complies, it is also impossible. God chose the man to be the leader in the home. He created man first, then the woman. Men need to hear the direction from Jesus and then call out *that* rhythm to their families. When the man is in subjection to Christ, the woman can confidently be in subjection to the man.

> Husbands, love your wives, even as Christ also loved the church, and gave himself for it; That he might sanctify and cleanse it with the washing of water by the word, That he might present it to himself a glorious church, not having spot, or wrinkle, or any such thing; but that it should be holy and without blemish. So men ought to love their wives as their own bodies. He that loveth his wife loveth himself.
>
> —Ephesians 5:25–28

The responsibility of the husband in marriage is a tremendous one. He is to give himself up for the sake of bringing his wife into the woman she was created to be. He is to lead the home in the ways of the Lord. When the husband does his part, it is easy for the woman to come alongside with support for him and to submit to the leadership he provides. She can then feel confident in her position. Her part is no less important. She is never said to be a silent partner. She brings balance to her husband. Each works for the good of the other.

This is God's order. If either mate falls short of the order God has set up, it causes imbalance and confusion. Marriage according to God's plan cannot be possible if there is intermarriage between a Christian and non-Christian. How can two work together when one's commander is the Lord God and the other's is the world? In the Old Testament they were strictly forbidden to marry outside the Jewish culture. In speaking of the heathen nations, God spoke this to Israel:

> Neither shalt thou make marriages with them; thy daughter thou shalt not give unto his son, nor his daughter shalt thou take unto thy son. For they will turn away thy son from following me, that they may serve other gods: so will the anger of the Lord be kindled against you, and destroy thee suddenly.
>
> —DEUTERONOMY 7:3–4

What was the reason for this commandment? The heathen wives led their husbands away from truth and taught their children idolatry.

The same order is upheld under the new covenant. "Be ye not unequally yoked together with unbelievers: for what fellowship hath righteousness with unrighteousness? and what communion hath light with darkness?" (2 Cor. 6:14). Jesus went among those who were sinners and in need in order to change their hearts and their circumstances on many occasions, but He did not come into agreement with them. Neither are we to come into agreement (as in marriage or even business partnerships) with those who are unbelievers. We do not share the same principles. It is not impossible to have a marriage between a believer and an unbeliever, but it is impossible to have a marriage according to God's order when one is a believer and one is not. One partner has the principles of the world and lives by them. The other has the principles of Christ and lives by them. This clash of lifestyles can cause division and ungodly compromise on the part of the believer. We have many such marriages today because we have not been taught God's order. God's people need instruction.

What do you do if you are already in that position? First Corinthians 7:10–13 deals clearly with marriages between believers and unbelievers.

> And unto the married I command, yet not I, but the Lord, Let not the wife depart from her husband: But and if she depart, let her remain unmarried or be reconciled to her husband: and let not the husband put away his wife. But to the rest speak I, not the Lord: If any brother hath a wife that believeth not, and she be pleased to dwell with him, let him not put her away. And the woman which hath an husband that believeth

not, and if he be pleased to dwell with her, let her
not leave him.

These marriages are not to be terminated unless the
unbelieving one is not willing to live with the believer.
The union of Christ and His church is an everlasting
union. The union of a man and his wife is until the death
of one of the partners.

> For the woman which hath an husband is bound
> by the law to her husband so long as he liveth;
> but if the husband be dead, she is loosed from the
> law of the husband. So then if, while her husband
> liveth, she be married to another man, she shall be
> called an adulteress: but if her husband be dead,
> she is free from that law; so that she is no adul-
> teress, though she be married to another man.
> —ROMANS 7:2–3

Jesus defined *adultery* like this. "It hath been said, Whosoever shall put away his wife, let him give her a writing of
divorcement: But I say unto you, That whosoever shall put
away his wife, saving for the cause of fornication, causeth
her to commit adultery: and whosoever shall marry her that
is divorced committeth adultery" (Matt. 5:31–32).

He speaks of this again in Mark 10:2–12:

> And the Pharisees came to him, and asked him, Is
> it lawful for a man to put away his wife? tempting
> him. And he answered and said unto them, What

did Moses command you? And they said, Moses suffered to write a bill of divorcement, and to put her away. And Jesus answered and said unto them, For the hardness of your heart he wrote you this precept. But from the beginning of the creation God made them male and female. For this cause shall a man leave his father and mother, and cleave to his wife; And they twain shall be one flesh: so then they are no more twain, but one flesh. What therefore God hath joined together, let not man put asunder. And in the house his disciples asked him again of the same matter. And he saith unto them, Whosoever shall put away his wife, and marry another, committeth adultery against her. And if a woman shall put away her husband, and be married to another, she committeth adultery.

Why, then, is there so much divorce and remarriage in the church? Good question. We have disregarded God's order. There is a lack of teaching in the church. The world's view projects that happiness comes from marriage (or living together) and God wants us to be happy. Because we have taken the world's view, many people divorce and remarry and, instead of gaining happiness, create situations that are totally confusing. This may be common among unbelievers but should not be common among Christians. Truly, God wants us to have joy, but true joy is contingent on following His order.

Many Christians have not been taught God's commandments concerning marriage and have become entangled in some very complicated circumstances. Others may have failed to follow God's order because they were not born again and had no knowledge or regard for His commandments at that time in their lives. Later they may want to follow in God's ways and seek His lordship. Where do they go from there? They can study the Word of God concerning their situation and see what God says. He will speak to their hearts and make His Word clear if they sincerely seek His truth.

Marriage vows are made before God and to one another. They are a sacred trust. God has a wonderful plan for marriage, and if we will follow His order, it works and is a beautiful relationship. Our families are worth fighting for. They are worth the effort it takes to have a godly marriage.

The God who created this universe, who created you and me, set up a design for marriage that still stands today. We are accountable for walking in the light of God's Word that has been shone into our hearts. If others compromise and condone what God has condemned or condemn what God has blessed, it will not change the standard by which we will all be judged when we stand before our great Creator. We will not stand before Him as a group, but as individuals. If we do not know the truth, we will fall into sin because of our ignorance. When we know what is right and don't do it, it is sin.

chapter 4

The Family

THE FAMILY IS a sacred institution created by God. Our society is on the brink of completely dismantling the family as God designed it. If they succeed, our society will fall. Chaos will reign. The whole of the civilized world is built on the integrity of the family unit. Each component is important to the whole. In the family we first learn of authority, loving, responsibility, sharing, and working together toward a common goal. Imagine how cold the world would be without the warmth and closeness of family. We are losing that valuable heritage at an alarming rate.

God's order for the family is perfect. As those born in sin, we cannot attain it without His Holy Spirit to empower us. We may not be perfect in every aspect, but we can learn what is expected and strive toward that mark. God's order brings harmony first in the individual between God and man. That harmony spills over into relationships in the family and even further to those outside the family. Each person within the family unit has a part to play in bringing about this balance of unity.

Husband/Father

The husband/father is to be the authority in the home. He is the president of the company (home) but not the owner. He answers to Jesus Christ and is held accountable as to how he supervises the other employees (wife and children). The president's closest confidante is his vice president (wife). His first priority is being in right relationship with the Owner (Jesus Christ). Then he can administrate the company in an efficient way.

Joshua chose the direction of his whole household. He had led the people of Israel into the Promised Land and had been their leader for many years. Obviously, he had ordered his family well, too. In his last gathering with the leadership of the various tribes, Joshua said:

> Now therefore fear the Lord, and serve him in sincerity and in truth: and put away the gods which your fathers served on the other side of the flood, and in Egypt; and serve the Lord. And if it seem evil unto you to serve the Lord, choose you this day whom ye will serve; whether the god which your fathers served that were on the other side of the flood, or the gods of the Amorites, in whose land ye dwell: but as for me and my house, we will serve the Lord.
>
> —Joshua 24:14–15

He was man enough to speak for his household. He had shown them the way. It is easy to say, "I am the head of this house." It is another to bring about what you claim. A leader is not a dictator. He is not infallible. He is not an island to himself in making decisions but seeks out wise counsel. He is godly. He is one who leans on the Lord and seeks Him with all his heart. He takes his position seriously—not just the honor of it but the responsibility as well. The husband's first responsibility is to be in right relationship with God. Until that happens, the other pieces of the puzzle will never fit.

A wise husband will not try to be the Lone Ranger and work everything out by himself. If he is wise, he will recognize the reason God has given him a wife. She is a *help* that is suitable for him. She is there to balance him in decision-making, aid him in family matters, and be a joy and strength to him.

The husband is to love his wife just as Christ loved the church. How much was that? Jesus gave Himself up for the church to make it what it should be so that it might be presented to Him "a glorious church, not having spot, or wrinkle, or any such thing; but that is should be holy and without blemish" (Eph. 5:27). When we give up ourselves for someone else, we find they will give themselves freely to us. Yes, the husband is the head. Although he has a partner, the final decision and responsibility is on his shoulders.

"So ought men to love their wives as their own bodies. He that loveth his wife loveth himself. For no man ever yet hated his own flesh; but nourisheth and cherisheth it, even as the Lord the church" (Eph. 5:28–29). Husbands are commanded to love their wives. They are commanded to give themselves up for their wives. A husband is to bring up his wife into the woman she is capable of becoming. He is to love her as he loves himself. If he does not honor his wife, his prayers can be hindered.

"Likewise, ye husbands, dwell with them according to knowledge, giving honour unto the wife, as unto the weaker vessel, and as being heirs together of the grace of life; that your prayers be not hindered" (1 Pet. 3:7). Giving honor is to value or esteem the wife in the highest degree. It is to value her abilities, her character, and her position.

The husband/father is to be the head authority in the home. Most people do not understand the nature of authority. They believe authority is the power to make people do whatever they decide. Mishandled authority is often seen showcased in front of others as proof of the power they possess. Everyone *under* them knows that they have the power to make or break them, because they believe ruling with an iron fist is the only way to make others obey. Those who throw their weight around just because they can are abusers. Authority is not domination.

Authority in the home, first of all, means the husband/father is *under* the authority of Christ. If he is not following God's order for the role of husband and father, he will have a home of confusion and disorder. His authority entails a responsibility to oversee the home. He is to be aware of the needs of his family (physically, mentally, financially, spiritually, and emotionally) and to provide for those needs.

"But if any provide not for his own, and specially for those of his own house, he hath denied the faith, and is worse than an infidel" (1 Tim. 5:8). A lazy man will bring shame and poverty to his family. A wise man will shoulder the charge God has given him. He will take care to see that all matters are handled. He may delegate some of the work, but the ultimate responsibility is his. In order to accomplish this responsibility, he must be submitted to God, and he needs to corroborate with the woman God has given him to help him.

If the husband/father is not in right relationship with God, his spiritual protection over his family is similar to an umbrella full of holes in a rainstorm. He will be totally inadequate, and his family will pay the price for his negligence.

Parents are responsible for the spiritual training of their children. The children are to be primarily taught in the home to follow the Lord's order. If they are trained in God's order from infancy, they can pattern their lives in accordance to His Word and not have the difficulty many have who do not know or understand God's order until they are older.

Deuteronomy 6 shows us the way to train them. "And these words, which I command thee this day, shall be in thine heart" (v. 6). Notice that before we can teach our children, God's Word must be active in us. "And thou shalt teach them diligently unto thy children, and shalt talk of them when thou sittest in thine house, and when thou walkest by the way, and when thou liest down, and when thou risest up" (v. 7).

The word *teach* means "to engrave God's principles on their hearts." If I take a pin and softly scratch my name on a piece of your furniture, you could sand it a little and buff it off. But if I took a knife and cut deep into the furniture, it would be there to stay. No matter how much you sanded or buffed, you could not remove it. That is how unrelentingly we are to be in teaching God's principles to our children—both by word and example. When our children are put in a position of worldly temptation, the Word within them will show them the way, both in their youth and until their old age. Speaking of Jesus and His teachings should be a natural thing for us. We should daily be applying spiritual truths to everyday situations at home, when we are riding down the road, when we go to bed at night, and when we get up in the morning. His commandments and truths should ever be before us, and it is the parents' duty to implant that firmly into their children's lives. In order to teach in this capacity, there must be a consistent godly lifestyle presented to our children every day and in all situations.

Ephesians 6:4 gives this warning: "And, ye fathers, provoke not your children to wrath: but bring them up in the nurture and admonition of the Lord." This caution is also found in Colossians 3:21. If parents are overbearing and require things of their children they do not emulate themselves, the children will become discouraged, bitter, and rebellious. Fathers need to have the principles of God in their hearts and active in their lives. What they say to teach their children will be overshadowed by what they do. If they are angry and bitter, their children will follow that example more quickly than their words of instruction telling them to be calm and loving. If we see undesirable behavior from our children, it may be a red flag for us to examine our behavior. Are we the example they are following, or is it some outside influence that needs to be dealt with? Will we execute all of this perfectly every time? Probably not. When we make a mistake, it is best to admit it, straighten it out if we can, and keep going in the right direction. It is important that children learn to admit (confess) mistakes and make them right, and seeing us handle these situations can teach them that lesson.

It is of great importance for parents to break any iniquitous traits that may have been passed down *to* them so they will not be passed down *through* them. It is possible for those traits to be transmitted from generation to generation.

> The LORD, The LORD God, merciful and gracious, longsuffering, and abundant in goodness and truth, keeping mercy for thousands, forgiving iniquity and transgression and sin, and that will by no means clear the guilty; visiting the iniquity of the fathers upon the children, and upon the children's children, unto the third and to the fourth generation.
>
> —EXODUS 34:6–7

It has always amazed me to hear statistics say that abused children usually become abusive parents. It seems it would be just the opposite. If a child is abused, one would think that, knowing the pain it causes, they would want to stay away from any form of abuse. Yet, what we see and experience has more influence than what we are told. Some families come to accept such behavior as normal and think it happens in all families. Drunkenness, lust, greed, lying, stubbornness, anger, witchcraft, and rebellion are just a few sins that can be passed down from generation to generation. The only way to break them is to confess and repent. Evil ways and sins that have been committed can influence many generations to come, until one is enlightened to the truth and stands up to break the chains of wickedness over their family. They resolve to say, "No, not me. As for me and my house, we will serve the Lord." This falls under the covering the husband/father is to provide for his household.

An examination of our own hearts can set generations to come at liberty. Just as evil can be passed down from parent to child, good can be the inheritance of children. A parent must follow Jesus before they can teach their child to follow Him.

Fathers, are you following God's order, or is your family huddled under an umbrella with holes while poverty, wickedness, ignorance of God's Word, and iniquity pours down on them? You can prevent these destructive elements from ruining your family simply by submitting to God's way. Maybe, up until now, you have not provided for them.

Wherever you may be, you can begin again. You can start over in submission to Christ.

WIFE/MOTHER

"Every wise woman buildeth her house: but the foolish plucketh it down with her hands" (Prov. 14:1). This passage is fascinating when you begin to meditate on it and see all the implications. The house is the family or the household. Women are not expected to build a physical house brick by brick but a household in which God's truth is believed and worked out step by step. The word *hands* in this scripture is for the open hand that denotes someone with the power, resources, and the direction to get the job done. Women have the power to build their homes or destroy them. Building is done by taking certain materials and putting them all in their proper places in order to make something. God has given women certain bricks that will build their family into a godly, orderly household. Those who are wise will take these bricks and begin building. On the other hand, the foolish will not learn what these bricks are, nor will they put them into place in their homes. Instead of building, they destroy. They pull down every family member and bring ruin in their lives. There is no order in tearing down, but there is in building up.

For those who want to know God's order for the women of the house, the bricks are listed in Titus 2:3–5:

> The aged women likewise, that they be in behaviour as becometh holiness, not false accusers, not

> given to much wine, teachers of good things; That they may teach the young women to be sober, to love their husbands, to love their children, To be discreet, chaste, keepers at home, good, obedient to their own husbands, that the word of God be not blasphemed.

That is more information than anyone can digest in one bite, so we need to break it down. It takes time to build brick by brick, but it gets the job done.

The older women are to teach the younger women how to build their homes. But, first, the older women need to be worthy to teach them. If their behavior is not characteristic of holiness, they are not to be given consideration.

Brick 1, "Be Sober"

That simply means that the builder needs wisdom that comes only from God in the context that her mind is free of intoxicants. If you are intoxicated, you are off balance, giddy, and irrational. Taking on the world's reasoning and attitudes will get us off balance. That is not clear, sound thinking but rather is thinking from a mind darkened to the things of God's Spirit. A woman who wants to build rather than tear down will have the mind of the Spirit regardless of the popular worldview. The Word of God and leadership of the Holy Spirit (who never goes against His written Word) have the final say in every situation in life whether natural feelings agree or disagree. If we try to think a situation through with the world's view, we turn our backs on God's order. Human rationalization keeps the mind from being spiritually alert to see situations clearly and make right decisions. A woman who is sober minded will influence everyone in her household (and outside of it) by her godly wisdom and stability. There is security in having a sound mind.

Brick 2, "Love Their Husbands"

Love is more than emotional fluff. Emotional fluff may play in the picture, but it is not ever-present in a husband/wife relationship. It comes and goes. That does not mean love comes and goes. Love involves affection, caring, and giving. One of the best ways to make the love of a wife for her husband clear is to look at Proverbs 31:10–12. A wife who loves her husband will seek his good and will help him succeed.

> Who can find a virtuous woman? for her price is far above rubies. The heart of her husband doth safely trust in her, so that he shall have no need of spoil. She will do him good and not evil all the days of her life.

Now, let's see what this verse is saying of the wife who is following God's order. She is "a virtuous woman"—a woman with a treasure chest of resources such as strength, power, riches, substance, and valor. Her value is much more than any earthly wealth. When a family member has a need, she can reach into the treasure chest and pull out whatever is needed for the situation. Her inner resources come from the Lord, the source of all strength and wisdom.

"The heart of her husband doth safely trust in her." Her husband can trust her to be faithful, to be responsible, and to prepare a home that is a place of refuge and security. The woman sets the tone in the home. She can make the home a haven, a torture chamber, or something in between. She should make the atmosphere one of confidence and genuine love. If the wife/mother is always agitated, the whole family will be agitated. If she is calm, the other family members will sense her calmness and relax. That should tell us something about the power women have in the home. Make it a place of refuge. The home should be a place where there is peace, unity, and safety; where there is understanding and no need to fear failures being uncovered; where there is joy when one is successful and happiness in being together; where there is trust, confidence, and hope.

"So that he shall have no need of spoil." In other words, his needs are met. The wife completes the husband, not competes with him. They may not always agree, but as they discuss the issues, they will bring balance to one another. Even in disagreements, the husband should be confident that his wife's objective is to build him up not to bring him down. Love sometimes involves telling someone they are wrong, but even that can be done in a tactful, supportive way.

"She will do him good and not evil." The wife is never to do anything that will bring shame to her husband.

Remember Abigail? She was married to a man named Nabal. His name meant *fool,* and he lived up to it. First Samuel 25 describes this couple like this: "She was a woman of good understanding, and of a beautiful countenance: but the man was churlish and evil in his doings" (v. 3). He was a cruel, obstinate man with no sense of justice or decency. He refused to show David and his men even a small kindness after they had done much to help him. David gathered his men, and they were on their way to kill Nabal, when they were met by Abigail. She had not told Nabal what she was going to do but brought them food and an explanation that kept them from killing her husband. It seems that Nabal did not deserve a wife like Abigail. When she returned, he was drunk, so she waited until morning to tell him what had happened. It staggered the heart of Nabal when he realized what danger he had been in. Before long Nabal was smitten of the Lord and died. Eventually, Abigail became David's wife. Although Abigail had a difficult husband who seems to have been just the opposite of her character, she did not do him evil. She did nothing to add shame to her husband.

Wives are to do nothing to bring a stumbling block to their husbands, either. They need to support them and help them in every way. A virtuous woman is quick to open that treasure chest for her husband and let him benefit from her resources.

"All the days of her life." Fairytales always end with "and they lived happily ever after." Another interpretation of that is "day–in and day–out." Married life is not always exciting.

It is not all walking through fields of flowers holding hands with a breeze blowing gently through your hair. Neither is it always dancing in the moonlight to romantic music. Life is day–in and day–out, day–in and day–out. It is important to keep doing what is good and right even when we don't feel like it, even in the everydayness of life. The husband of a godly woman does not need to fear his wife will abandon him if things become difficult. Women are to love their husbands consistently and seek their best.

Brick 3, "To Love Their Children"

Loving our children involves giving them the best we have. Love will give them the truth to base their lives on. It is a popular stance to let the children decide what they want to believe, but that is not what God said.

Both parents are responsible for the spiritual training of their children. They are to be taught in the home to follow the Lord's order. Deuteronomy 6 applies as much to the mother as to the father. A mother should train the children up to be wise, responsible, and caring, as well as teaching them how to become good husbands, wives, and parents. When a parent teaches their child, they are actually teaching future generations as well, for we tend to follow the principles we are taught.

Brick 4, "Be Discreet"

Discreet in this passage means "to be self-controlled." We could all use some improvement in an area or two on this one. Some need to work on their temper, some on following fads, spending, wasting time, etc. The areas where we are the weakest will probably be the areas of weakness in our family. We influence one another, and we need to strive to be a good example.

Being discreet also involves being consistent. Double-mindedness is a snare for our souls. If we have one set of rules for ourselves and another for everyone else, or if we compromise God's commandments when it will cost us to keep them, we are inconsistent and put forth a bad example that our children are sure to follow. We need to believe God and stick with what He says without letting the outer influences bring confusion. In James 1:8 we are told, "A double minded man is unstable in all his ways." If we are constantly wavering in what we believe, we will be unstable in everything we do in life. The problem comes when God's order is not favorable to us. If Jesus' teachings oppose our desires and expectations or if they cause us discomfort or hardship, we begin to rethink what we should do. That is a mistake. It causes confusion that, if entertained in our minds, will lead us away from Jesus. If the wife/mother is cold and indifferent to the call of Jesus, the family will probably follow. If she is consistent in her loyalty to Christ, they will follow that influence.

Brick 5, "Chaste"

Women according to God's order are to keep themselves innocent and pure from any carnality. They are to be modest in everything. A modest woman is not given to extremes. She is balanced—not too much and not too little. If her clothing, movements, words, and actions are immodest, she may get attention; but is it the kind of attention that is really favorable? Probably not. We usually think of clothing when we think of modesty, and, certainly, that is a big part. Our society has done away with decency in dress, speech, and actions. There is no shame on the faces of those involved in unchaste, immodest behavior. Proverbs 7:6–23 describes the brazenness of a woman who is unchaste and boisterous. These women ruin the lives, hearts, and souls of men. They behave just the opposite of God's order for women.

The godly woman is not to partake of such behavior. Modesty does not draw attention to the outward person. First Peter 3 speaks of real beauty being that of the heart, "a meek and quiet spirit, which is in the sight of God of great price" (v. 4).

Brick 6, "Keepers at Home"

Women are to keep their homes. They need to be good housekeepers and domestically inclined in order to care for their families. They also need to be the guard of the house. We have alarm systems to detect fires, theft, and a myriad of other intruders that will bring injury to our families. The wife is to be on guard of other intruders that come to wreck the lives of everyone in the house. These intruders come in the guise of entertainment, such as: television programs, radio, books, magazines, and computers. These trespassers steal our time and our minds. Even good things can be harmful when overdone. Then there are the attitudes, words, and actions that are detrimental to the family's spiritual welfare. These need to be detected and eliminated while they are just a vapor of smoke rather than a raging fire. It takes discernment and timely response to be the keeper at home. Here are a few helpful hints in keeping your home free from danger.

1. Don't let the sun go down on your wrath. If there is a disagreement or harsh words, don't let reconciliation wait until another day. Make it right. Even if you still don't agree, agree to disagree. Plan to work on the problem but not to be angry with one another.

2. Don't stifle feelings until you have stuffed so many problems inside that you eventually explode. Talk about problems freely and resolve them while they are only roots. If you develop a root of bitterness within and leave it alone, it will spring up and cause major problems later involving many.

3. Don't give Satan a toehold in your life. Don't get too personal with another man (or husbands with another woman). Flirting is wrong unless it's with your spouse. Situations where men and women work closely together need to be guarded and possibly eliminated if there is even a hint of a problem.

4. Encourage one another and strengthen one another. There is enough in the world to tear us down without bringing it into the home.

5. Watch your words. It is easy to become cruel with our words during disagreements. Even if you have been mistreated, be careful how you approach your mate and what you say.

Brick 7, "Good"

One who is good in character is beneficial to those whose lives they touch. If we live well, we enhance the lives of others. A wife and mother will be a godly influence on her children and husband. She will bring the balance, strength, and goodness they need to please the Lord.

Brick 8, "Obedient to Their Own Husbands"

The wife is to be in subjection to her husband. The head of the woman is the man. What if he is not a godly man? First Peter 3:1–4 says:

> Likewise ye wives, be in subjection to your own husbands; that, if any obey not the word, they also may without the word be won by the conversation of the wives; While they behold your chaste conversation coupled with fear. Whose adorning let it not be that outward adorning of plaiting the hair, and of wearing of gold, or of putting on of apparel; but let it be the hidden man of the heart, in that which is not corruptible, even the ornament of a meek and quiet spirit, which is in the sight of God of great price.

A woman with an ungodly husband does not have to preach to him but should live the gospel before him every day. The word *conversation* means "behavior," not "words." They will not be won into the kingdom by lectures (husbands call this nagging) or by the outward beauty of their wives, but they can be won by godly character and a beautiful heart.

All women should be models—not fashion models, but an example for their children and others to follow. D. L. Moody was said to have prayed that his daughters would be famous in God's kingdom. Oh, that we would live in such a way that all our children would be famous in the kingdom of God. The fame of this world is temporary and deceitful, but fame in the heavenly sphere has endless rewards.

Now, women, are you pulling down bricks from your home, or are you building it up a little more every day? Those who do not become the woman of God's order are pulling bricks out of their house one at a time. It may seem things are just fine for a while, but the crumbling effect will become evident before long. It may be subtle at first, and it seems being slack toward God's principles is not really making a difference. But eventually the whole house will collapse into a pile around their feet. Even at that point, a woman can begin the building process by taking hold of the principles of God and implementing them in her life.

If you realize you have been pulling bricks out of your home, you can stop that process immediately and begin to replace them. It is not too late to begin undoing the damage that has been done, but you must remember it will take time and consistency. You *can* influence your household for good.

The atmosphere of the home is in the woman's hands. And the atmosphere can produce creativity, faithfulness, responsibility, godliness, and all the other good qualities needed to make a happy, fulfilled life. She can build brick by brick as she is and acts like the woman God has designed her to be.

Children

God's order reaches out to the children, too. They have a responsibility toward the parents. "Children, obey your parents in the Lord: for this is right. Honour thy father and mother; which is the first commandment with promise; That it may be well with thee, and thou mayest live long on the earth" (Eph. 6:1–3). Obedience is necessary if the child is to learn godly principles. Just as teaching and training are the duties of the parents, attentiveness and compliance are the duties of the children. Obedience includes listening attentively as a subordinate and then conforming to the commands of the authority. Honor is recognizing the value of the person, the authority, and the commandments. Children need to know who is in charge. Each member of the family needs to understand their place and fulfill their own responsibilities.

> My son, keep thy father's commandment, and forsake not the law of thy mother: Bind them continually upon thine heart, and tie them about

thy neck. When thou goest, it shall lead thee;
when thou sleepest, it shall keep thee; and when
thou awakest, it shall talk with thee. For the
commandment is a lamp; and the law is light; and
reproofs of instruction are the way of life.

—Proverbs 6:20–24

Remember the duties of the parents in Deuteronomy 6 to engrave God's principles in the children's hearts? This Proverb is the children's counterpart of that passage.

Honoring parents is listening to their instruction, upholding their teachings, and receiving their correction. If the child is rebellious and will not keep the rules of the house, they can expect punishment. They need to learn how to be under authority and show respect to their parents even when they disagree with them. Sometimes parents may punish mistakenly, just like the children may make mistakes in obeying. Good parents will chastise when necessary *for the good of the child*, not because they need to vent their anger.

Furthermore we have had fathers of our flesh
which corrected us, and we gave them reverence:
shall we not much rather be in subjection unto
the Father of spirits, and live? For they verily for
a few days chastened us after their own pleasure;
but he for our profit, that we might be partakers
of his holiness.

—Hebrews 12:9–10

Compliance to the right leadership in the home will produce children of strength, honor, and integrity. When children are unruly, it is because of a breakdown of God's order, either with the parents or the children. God's system (when followed) brings order in the home, both in the husband-wife relationship as well as the parent-child relationship. It is the children's responsibility to be pliable and in subjection to the leadership in the home. They are commanded by God to obey. When they are disobedient and rebellious, it brings a reproach on their parents rather than honor. "A wise son maketh a glad father: but a foolish man despiseth his mother" (Prov. 15:20).

If a child is a Christian and the parents are not, they are not to treat their parents with dishonor. "Whoso curseth his father or his mother, his lamp shall be put out in obscure darkness" (Prov. 20:20).

As the children grow up and leave home, they take on the responsibility for their own family. "Therefore shall a man leave his father and his mother, and shall cleave unto his wife: and they shall be one flesh" (Gen. 2:24). Even so, they still have a responsibility toward their parents. "If any widow have children or nephews, let them learn first to shew piety at home, and to requite their parents: for that is good and acceptable before God....But if any provide not for his own, and specially for those of his own house [kindred], he hath denied the faith, and is worse than an infidel" (1 Tim. 5:4, 8). When the parents become aged and need help, it is the responsibility of the children to see to their care. This is very clear. This is God's order.

Jesus was plain about this principle when He spoke out against the self-serving traditions of the scribes and Pharisees.

> Full well ye reject the commandment of God, that ye may keep your own tradition. For Moses said, Honour thy father and thy mother; and, Whoso curseth father or mother, let him die the death: But ye say, If a man shall say to his father or mother, It is Corban, that is to say, a gift, by whatsoever thou mightest be profited by me; he shall be free. And ye suffer him no more to do ought for his father or his mother; Making the word of God of none effect through your tradition, which ye have delivered: and many such like things do ye.
>
> —MARK 7:9–13

The Pharisees had a way to get around supporting their parents. They would swear by the gold of the temple and the gift on the altar in a vow that would release them from assisting their parents. By their little tradition they were free from the burden of support as they vowed all their worldly goods to God. But this did not free them in God's eyes. Jesus said they were rejecting the commandment of God so they could keep their own traditions. Those who did not care for and honor their parents were to "die the death." By their disobedience to God's Word, they were "making the word of God of none effect."

These religious men were more eager to impress their

peers and the people with their so-called selfless giving to the Lord than to keep the commandment of God to honor and take care of their aging parents. They were more caught up in the prestige and power of their positions than in the actual keeping of God's Law. They were in essence robbing their parents. They were ignoring their responsibility. "Whoso robbeth his father or his mother, and saith, It is no transgression; the same is the companion of a destroyer" (Prov. 28:24). It is a spiritual thing to obey God's commandments in practical ways.

Even Jesus, as He hung on the cross, did not forget His mother. He made provision from the cross for John to care for His mother. Jesus was the oldest child and the responsibility was His. He honored His mother. "Hearken unto thy father that begat thee, and despise not thy mother when she is old" (Prov. 23:22).

There is never a time when family ceases to be responsible for one another. As the children grow up and the parents grow old, the responsibilities change, but we are always held accountable. It is a duty, an obligation, and a privilege to care for one another. It is the order of God.

chapter 5

The Fall

So, GOD CREATED everything with harmony between the animals, Adam, Eve, and Himself. He also instituted marriage and the family. They had perfect peace with God because there was no barrier of sin between them. They had open, unhindered fellowship with God on a daily basis.

"And they were both naked, the man and his wife, and were not ashamed" (Gen. 2:25). How many people do you know who are transparent in their spirit? Most people have something they want to hide from the eyes of others. It may be greed, lust, manipulation, lies, disobedience, hatred, a checkered past, or any number of other things. Before sin entered the world, there was no need for a cover-up. There was nothing evil because man had been made in God's image and sin had not been brought into the picture. There was nothing in man to cloud the image of God there.

God gave specific instructions to Adam in this paradise: "And the LORD God commanded the man, saying, Of every tree of the garden thou mayest freely eat: But of the tree of the knowledge of good and evil, thou shalt not eat of it: for in the day that thou eatest thereof thou shalt surely die" (Gen. 2:16–17). I don't know how long Adam and Eve lived in the garden in obedience to God's command. The Bible does not say how long the age of innocence lasted before Eve gave in to the temptation of Satan. But, regardless how long they enjoyed perfection, they eventually fell into the snare of the devil.

Before we can understand the fall of mankind, we must have an understanding of who Satan is. We must know there is an evil power at work in the world, but Satan was not always evil. He began as an angel of God, created by God in beauty and with musical ability to send up worship to God.

> Thou hast been in Eden the garden of God; every precious stone was thy covering....The workmanship of thy tabrets and of thy pipes was prepared in thee in the day that thou wast created. Thou art the anointed cherub that covereth; and I have set thee so: thou wast upon the holy mountain of God; thou hast walked up and down in the midst of the stones of fire. Thou wast perfect in thy ways from the day that thou wast created, till iniquity was found in thee.
>
> —Ezekiel 28:13–15

If Satan was created in such a perfect fashion, how did he become such a diabolical opponent of God? Iniquity was found in him. Iniquity is the same as evil. Our word *iniquity* comes from two Latin words, *not* and *equal*.

When iniquity is found in someone, they are not equal to the wholeness and perfection in which God created everything. They are far less than what God made. Imperfection (evil) has entered in and disrupted the order of God. However, as we will see in coming chapters, this interruption of God's order is only temporary.

Isaiah 14:12–15 explains the details of Satan's fall:

> How art thou fallen from heaven, O Lucifer, son of the morning! how art thou cut down to the ground, which didst weaken the nations! For thou hast said in thine heart, I will ascend into heaven, I will exalt my throne above the stars of God: I will sit also upon the mount of the congregation, in the sides of the north: I will ascend above the heights of the clouds; I will be like the most High. Yet thou shalt be brought down to hell, to the sides of the pit.

And in Ezekiel 28:17 it tells us more:

> Thine heart was lifted up because of thy beauty, thou hast corrupted thy wisdom by reason of thy brightness: I will cast thee to the ground, I will lay thee before kings, that they may behold thee.

Lucifer's heart was filled with himself, and in his pride he boasted of what he would do. He intended to exalt himself above God, but no one will ever succeed in such an endeavor. When we are filled with ourselves, we are filled with pride. Proverbs 16:18 says, "Pride goeth before destruction, and an haughty spirit before a fall."

Since the time pride and rebellion rose up in Satan and he was cast out of Heaven, he became the leading adversary of God and has led many people astray. His cunning is most deceitful, as he can make lies sound so true. This is the creature that felled mankind, and he will pay the price of his rebellion in the end.

Satan took a third of the angels with him in his rebellion. They are the evil spirits used in Satan's order (actually, disorder) of things. Jude 6 refers to the angels who left their first estate. "And the angels which kept not their first estate, but left their own habitation, he hath reserved in everlasting chains under darkness unto the judgment of the great day." Second Peter 2:4 mentions those angels that sinned. In a list of times when God brought judgment we read: "For if God spared not the angels that sinned, but cast them down to hell, and delivered them into chains of darkness, to be reserved unto judgment." Verse 9 continues, "The Lord knoweth how to deliver the godly out of temptations, and to reserve the unjust unto the day of judgment to be punished." Satan himself will be punished forever. "And the devil that deceived them was cast into the lake of fire and brimstone, where the beast and the false prophet are, and shall be tormented day and night for ever and ever" (Rev. 20:10).

Satan's character is the opposite of God's character. Satan is a liar. Jesus said to certain Jews who did not believe, "Ye are of your father the devil, and the lusts of your father ye will do. He was a murderer from the beginning, and abode not in the truth, because there is no truth in him. When he speaketh a lie, he speaketh of his own: for he is a liar, and the father of it" (John 8:44). When works have to be done in darkness, they are evil. When the truth has to be hidden, something is wrong. Jesus was plain in speaking the truth whether it was received or rejected. He *is* the truth. Jesus is Light and makes all things clear. There is "no variableness, neither shadow of turning" in God (James 1:17). He is pure Light and cannot cast even a shadow of darkness.

Satan turned from the truth, and the only other way to go is to a lie. He is a deceiver. In order to lead others into his deceit, he will transform himself into an angel of light, pretending to be holy. Those who do his bidding as false apostles and teachers also pretend to be godly followers of Christ (2 Cor. 11:13–15). When just enough truth is projected to make a doctrine seem credible or scriptural, many people can be deceived by it. But half-truth is not truth. Half-truth casts a shadow of darkness.

That is the bait Satan used to lure Eve and to deceive her. He came to her in the form of a serpent and asked about God's command not to eat of the tree. He told Eve, "Ye shall not surely die: For God doth know that in the day ye eat thereof, then your eyes shall be opened, and ye shall be as gods, knowing good and evil" (Gen. 3:4–5). This put a question in Eve's mind. Could they have more than they already possessed by eating that fruit? Was God keeping something good from them? The fruit didn't seem dangerous. It was beautiful to look at, so she indulged. God could have kept them from eating the fruit, but He gave them a choice, a free will, to do as they desired. We are not pre-programmed robots but thinking individuals with a will of our own to decide to do right or wrong.

Eve ate and gave some to Adam. "And the eyes of them both were opened, and they knew that they were naked; and they sewed fig leaves together, and made themselves aprons" (Gen. 3:7). Their eyes were open to know evil, and rather than becoming like God, they became slaves to sin. Something within them died. They changed. The change was obvious to them, and it was frightening. They were afraid to face God. That had never happened before.

Rather than a nature of pure innocence, suddenly a sin nature entered Adam and Eve. They were created in God's image, but they invited something inside of them that was totally against God's character. Where their minds had been enlightened to spiritual things, they became darkened (carnal). Where they had walked in innocence, they became guilty of sin. Even their bodies began the process of decline, bodies that were created to live forever.

From that moment on, the children produced were born with that sin nature, capable of committing every heinous sin imaginable.

> This is the book of the generations of Adam. In the day that God created man, in the likeness of God made he him; Male and female created he them; and blessed them, and called their name

Adam, in the day when they were created. And
Adam lived an hundred and thirty years, and
begat a son in his own likeness, after his image;
and called his name Seth.

—Genesis 5:1–3

Everything God created was productive. Everything
worked together in perfect balance—the soil, plants, mist,
trees, animals, and people—until Satan intervened. But
God was not caught off guard. He was not wringing His
hands and wondering what He would do now that Satan
had made his move. God already had a plan to redeem
mankind before this ever happened. He would send a
Savior.

When God confronted Adam and Eve with their sin,
Adam passed the blame to Eve, who quickly passed the
blame to the serpent who had deceived her. God began to
pass judgment on them all.

The serpent was cursed to crawl on its belly and eat dust
all its life. But Genesis 3:15 gives the promise of Jesus:
"And I will put enmity between thee and the woman, and
between thy seed and her seed; it shall bruise thy head,
and thou shalt bruise his heel." Certainly it took the death
of Jesus to redeem the human race, but Jesus mortally
wounded Satan in the process.

The woman was cursed with pain and sorrow in child-
birth and was put in subjection to her husband for him to
rule over her.

Because of the man's sin, God cursed the ground to

bring up thorns and thistles. No longer would the tending of the earth be a joy, but it would become hard work. "In the sweat of thy face shalt thou eat bread, till thou return unto the ground; for out of it wast thou taken: for dust thou art, and unto dust shalt thou return" (Gen. 3:19). Work is not a curse. It was going on before the Fall. God "took the man, and put him into the Garden of Eden to dress it and to keep it" (Gen. 2:15). Adam was given a job. Work is not a result of the Fall. It has been made difficult, often unpleasant, and strenuous because of the Fall; but, work was instituted immediately after mankind was created. Adam's task was to serve in the garden and to attend to whatever needed to be done. He was also to protect it and guard it. We find he was negligent of this, as he allowed the curse to come upon all of creation because of his disobedience. His disobedience not only affected him, but every part of the earth.

> For the earnest expectation of the creature waiteth for the manifestation of the sons of God. For the creature was made subject to vanity, not willingly, but by reason of him who hath subjected the same in hope, Because the creature itself also shall be delivered from the bondage of corruption into the glorious liberty of the children of God. For we know that the whole creation [every creature] groaneth and travaileth in pain together until now. And not only they, but ourselves also, which have the firstfruits of the Spirit, even we ourselves

> groan within ourselves, waiting for the adoption,
> to wit, the redemption of our body.
>
> —Romans 8:19–23

We who are born again have the Spirit of God within us now, yet we live in this sin-cursed world. We groan and await the day when our bodies will be free from the gravity of sin that pulls constantly at us within and without. All of creation experiences the same curse and longs for redemption from it.

God, in His mercy, sent Adam and Eve out of the Garden of Eden and placed "Cherubims, and a flaming sword which turned every way, to keep the way of the tree of life" (Gen. 3:24). If they had eaten of the tree of life, they would have lived forever in this sinful, cursed, degenerate state. God loved them too much for that. It was better for the body to die and turn their spirits loose to serve Him than to live forever in sin.

Through the sin of pride, Satan grasped for the praise that belonged to God. He tried to usurp God's authority and take His glory. He failed. Satan was cast out of Heaven along with the angels who had joined in his rebellion. He then began to corrupt God's creation through temptation to commit sin.

Mankind's first sin was a longing for what was forbidden—a lust for knowledge of that which was evil. Adam and Eve had no knowledge of evil before. They only knew good. This temptation promised to open their eyes and make them like God, or as gods. The temptation offered the promise of something better, but it was a total deception. There *was* nothing better. So, Adam and Eve gave up paradise for sickness, pain, toil, and death.

We always lose when we get out of God's perimeters. He sets boundaries around that which is good and tells us to go no farther, much like we do our young children. But we want more. When we demand more and break from God's Word, we may get what we want, but we will reap destruction. The problem is, when we get what we want, we discover we don't really want it. God's order is the only safe place.

chapter 6

The Law

BECAUSE OF THE fall of mankind, God gave the Law. With their eyes opened to evil as well as good, people needed a standard to help them understand what things were right and which ones were unacceptable.

There is only one who can accurately and fairly make that judgment—the Lord God Jehovah. Before laws can be valid, they must be prescribed by someone with the authority and power to make the laws *and* uphold them, bringing good to those who obey and punishment to those who disobey. God gave the Law through Moses to the people of Israel. He gave many laws we can read in Exodus, Leviticus, and Deuteronomy. They were guidelines for lifestyle, relationships, and worship.

"Wherefore then serveth the law? It was added because of transgressions." (Gal. 3:19). Because of sin, God gave the Law to show us what sin is. He set up laws to obey and sacrifices that had to be made to cover people's sins. "What shall we say then? Is the law sin? God forbid. Nay, I had not known sin, but by the law: for I had not known lust, except the law had said, Thou shalt not covet" (Rom. 7:7). "For by the law is the knowledge of sin" (Rom. 3:20). Why was it important for God to give the Law illuminating our sin? Because we will not try to avoid sin or ask forgiveness for sin if we do not know what sin is and don't clearly understand its consequences. For lack of truth, we believe lies.

A small child doesn't know that fire is dangerous until someone tells them or they get hurt. God, in His great mercy, provides the Law for us so we don't have to be destroyed by sin. When parents tell their child that fire will hurt them, they are not trying to scare the child or threaten him or her. They are simply speaking the facts and giving him information so he can make better choices. The Law showed us sin so we could avoid it. The Law showed us the consequences of sin so we could choose life.

"Wherefore the law is holy, and the commandment holy, and just, and good" (Rom. 7:12). The view of goodness and holiness became blurred at the Fall. Where only a sense of goodness and knowledge of goodness had prevailed, a sense of evil and knowledge of evil came into view, and the line between the two meshed. God had to make clear distinction between good and evil and make a way for sins to be wiped away. The animal sacrifices served this purpose until the perfect Sacrifice came.

The Ten Commandments given by God to Moses on Mount Sinai are the most familiar and basic of the laws of God. They cover the general categories of every sin, while the numerous other laws are more specific in what constituted sin and what punishment was required. Many of God's laws were also for health and sanitation purposes.

> And God spake all these words, saying, I am the LORD thy God, which have brought thee out of the land of Egypt, out of the house of bondage.
> —EXODUS 20:1–2

God then began to give the Ten Commandments.

> [1.] Thou shalt have no other gods before me.
> — EXODUS 20:3

If we truly believe God is who He says He is, we know He is the Most High God. There is none above Him. In that case it would be very foolish to put anything above Him on our priority list. If we do not recognize His supremacy, the truth has eluded us. We must be careful that we do not begin to believe in God as we have created Him to be in our own minds rather than the God He is. That is erecting an idol to worship instead of worshiping the true God "in spirit and in truth" (John 4:24). We don't need to recreate God. He is perfect in every way. We cannot improve on His character, His works, or His words. To do so implies we believe there is something or someone greater than God. The beginning of the commandments starts with recognizing who God is—the very essence of who He is. If we do not believe that basic fact, we will turn from Him and put something or someone above Him.

[2.] Thou shalt not make unto thee any graven image, or any likeness of any thing that is in heaven above, or that is in the earth beneath, or that is in the water under the earth: thou shalt not bow down thyself to them, nor serve them: for I the Lord thy God am a jealous God, visiting the iniquity of the fathers upon the children unto the third and fourth generation of them that hate me; and shewing mercy unto thousands of them that love me, and keep my commandments.

—Exodus 20:4–6

We are not to worship anything or anyone but God. We may never consider worshiping an idol of wood or stone, but many things beckon us and draw us to give them preeminence in our lives—ideologies, riches, fame, position, power, religions, etc. Worship goes beyond words and songs. It is evident by the priorities we choose in our lives. We all put an emphasis on something. What is it? Is God the central focus of our lives around which everything else revolves, or is He just one aspect of our lives that we added to revolve around our major issue?

Becoming a Christian is not just adding another element to our lifestyle. Our lives do not go on as they have except that now we go to church and do church work. That is not Christianity. Jesus Christ changes the whole of our lives when we are born again. He changes who we are. If there has been no radical change within that spills over to the outside, there has been no salvation. Jesus doesn't put a patch on the places that are not suitable to Him and leave us on our own. He expects us to follow Him completely with a life that represents His character and authority. We cannot do that on our own. First John 5:21 says, "Little children, keep yourselves from idols." That simply means to keep ourselves from anything that would take the place of God in our lives. Those who walk in the Spirit will worship God alone.

> [3.] Thou shalt not take the name of the LORD thy God in vain; for the LORD will not hold him guiltless that taketh his name in vain.
> —EXODUS 20:7

If someone speaks the name of the Lord lightly and in a useless way, they are guilty of breaking this commandment. The Lord's name is His authority and His character and should not be used foolishly. Many use the name of the Lord in invoking curses on other people or things. Some use His name lightly, with a little Southern flavor, as in, "Oh, Lord, look how that child has grown!" Others use the name of Jesus as if they knew Him, yet they are not authorized to use His name because they do not serve Him.

Jesus spoke to His disciples about being one with Him and the Father. He said, "He that believeth on me, the works that I do shall he do also; and greater works than these shall he do: because I go unto my Father. And whatsoever ye shall ask in my name, that will I do, that the Father may be glorified in the Son. If ye shall ask any thing in my name, I will do it" (John 14:12–14). Many take that to mean just anyone can use Jesus' name as a sort of magic charm to get whatever they want. Remember, Jesus spoke of our being one with Him and the Father and believing on Him. Keep in mind that believing is not just a mental task but is placing our whole self on Jesus Christ, His Person, His works, and His message. When we are at one with Him, we will ask according to His will. Then we know He hears us and we have whatever we have asked of Him. (See 1 John 5:15.)

Using the name of Jesus carries with it a great responsibility. We must be careful not to use His name in a flitting manner for empty purposes. Permission is required to use a registered trademark. Those who use the name of Jesus must be followers of His. Don't take His name in vain. When I was in my early twenties, I heard of a godly woman who had cancer and was dying. I visited her home and took my guitar to play and sing some hymns with her. She was an elderly lady, and her time was almost over. Before I left her house, she gave me some advice that has never left me. She said, "Don't ever do anything to bring a reproach on the name of your Lord." We would all do well to follow that admonition. Hold His name in high esteem and reverence.

> [4.] Remember the sabbath day, to keep it holy. Six days shalt thou labour, and do all thy work: but the seventh day is the sabbath of the LORD thy God: in it thou shalt not do any work, thou, nor thy son, nor thy daughter, thy manservant, nor thy maidservant, nor thy cattle, nor thy stranger that is within thy gates: for in six days the LORD made heaven and earth, the sea, and all that in

them is, and rested the seventh day: wherefore the
Lord blessed the sabbath day, and hallowed it.
—Exodus 20:8–11

No work was to be done on the seventh day, which was set aside for rest. Every literal Sabbath was holy to the Lord. It was for the good of the people to rest their bodies and minds. It was a commandment of the Lord to be kept. It is still a good idea to have a day to rest our bodies and minds, but we seldom do it, even on Sunday. This commandment was fulfilled in Jesus. As Christians we have a spiritual Sabbath to keep. In Hebrews 4 we read about the rest God intended for His people. God had rested after He finished creating all that was created. It was finished. He wanted Israel to enter into His rest, this trust in Him, but they pursued their own ways. Verses 9 and 10 tell us of the rest He offers us today. "There remaineth therefore a rest [keeping of a sabbath] to the people of God. For he that is entered into his rest, he also hath ceased from his own works, as God did from his." (See also Isaiah 58:13–14.)

God invites us to keep the Sabbath rest by ceasing from our own works and taking on His will, His Spirit, and His works. It requires self-denial to do so, and few people keep this Sabbath. It is easier to observe every seventh day than to give ourselves wholly to Christ every day and allow Him to dictate our lives. Jesus was occasionally accused of breaking the Sabbath laws, but He is Lord of the Sabbath! He had perfect rest in the Father's will—not

His own works. "Let us labour therefore to enter into that rest, lest any man fall after the same example of unbelief [disobedience]" (Heb. 4:11). This rest is complete and quiet confidence in the Lord. It is easy when we know Him intimately, but difficult as long as we feel the need to be in control and struggle for our own way.

As my son was learning to drive, I realized I would rather do the driving myself than let him do it. We did not get there any faster when I drove, but I wanted to be in control and be active rather than sitting in the passenger's seat. Something in our human nature makes us feel like we are accomplishing more when we are active and in control, when we are planning and working it all out. As we mature in the Lord, we learn to lay it all in God's hands and rest.

"Let no man therefore judge you in meat, or in drink, or in respect of an holyday, or of the new moon, or of the sabbath days: which are a shadow of things to come; but the body is of Christ" (Col. 2:16–17). Many may keep Sunday as a day of rest but break God's Sabbath with worry, anxiety, and relying on their own works. This spiritual rest in God—putting our whole weight on Him—is true, pure rest. We can be confident that He will take the good along with the bad and work them for our good if we are the called according to His purposes. (See Romans 8:28.)

> [5.] Honour thy father and thy mother: that thy days may be long upon the land which the Lord thy God giveth thee.
>
> —Exodus 20:12

This commandment has a promise attached. We should have high regard for our parents and show them respect. Those who are ungodly or abusive may not *deserve* honor, but we still honor their position. That honor continues through the various stages of our lives. Ephesians 6:1 says, "Children, obey your parents in the Lord: for this is right." As children, we are to bend to their training and not rebel. We are to respect their position and be pliable. Of course, the parents have a responsibility here, too. They are to engrave on the hearts of every child the Word of the Lord by lifestyle as well as words. They are to refrain from provoking their children to anger. They are not to be the stimulus for resentment and bitterness. That only serves to discourage the child and cause rebellion. Parents are to bring up their children "in the nurture and admonition of the Lord" (Eph. 6:4).

Proverbs 23:22 tells us, "Hearken unto thy father that begat thee, and despise not thy mother when she is old." When parents become old and need assistance, the children are to continue honoring their parents and give them that assistance. "Honour widows that are widows indeed. But if any widow have children or nephews, let them learn first to shew piety at home, and to requite their parents: for that is good and acceptable before God. (1 Tim. 5:3–4). It is the full responsibility of the children to see to the care of their elderly parents. The word *requite* means "to repay." They took care of us when we were young. We are to care for them when they are old. This principle is taught in the Old and New Covenants.

[6.] Thou shalt not kill.

—Exodus 20:13

It is against God's law to take the life of another person. Jesus took this commandment a step farther. He said, "Ye have heard that it was said by them of old time, Thou shalt not kill; and whosoever shall kill shall be in danger of the judgment: But I say unto you, That whosoever is angry with his brother without a cause shall be in danger of the judgment: and whosoever shall say to his brother, Raca, shall be in danger of the council: but whosoever shall say, Thou fool, shall be in danger of hell fire" (Matt. 5:21–23). The act of murder begins in the heart. If the anger, jealousy and any other evil intent is dealt with when it is a seed in the heart, it will never grow into such a violent act. Most would not actually commit the physical act of murder, but it is in their heart because of a spirit of murder to which they yield although it is restrained anger.

Under the old covenant, the people tried to keep these laws on their own. It was proven that they could not do it because of their sin nature. Jesus came to point out that the problem was in the heart, and then He made a way to change the heart. When we are born again, we change on the inside, and that changes the outward behavior. Murder takes the life of another person into our own hands and is a terrible evil. If our hearts are free from anger, our feelings cannot grow into an act of murder.

[7.] Thou shalt not commit adultery.

—Exodus 20:14

Adultery is unfaithfulness to one's marriage vows when the spouse is still living. Jesus spoke of adultery as occurring in the heart before the act follows: "Ye have heard that it was said by them of old time, Thou shalt not commit adultery: But I say unto you, that whosoever looketh on a woman to lust after her hath committed adultery with her already in his heart" (Matt. 5:27–28). There are times when you cannot help what you see, but usually we see and hear what we choose. We can keep away from printed material that is explicit, as well as keeping our minds and eyes away from Web sites, television programs, movies, and other places where we would encounter such evil. There is enough sinful behavior, immodest dress, etc., thrust upon us in daily life without trying to find it. We do not have to let these things get a hold on our thoughts. If we do, that is the first step down. Adultery, as with murder, begins in the heart and mind. That spirit of adultery tries to enter and take control. We must be on guard against it. If our hearts are pure, our actions will be pure. Married people need to keep from becoming too close to those of the opposite sex in work relationships, at church, and any other situations. Make that choice ahead of time and stick with it. If we do not take the first step to familiarity, we will not have to worry about taking the second or third. It is always better to take the high road.

[8.] Thou shalt not steal.

—Exodus 20:15

When one steals, they take something that does not belong to them. The Hebrew word here means "to deceive or thieve," so to obtain an item by deception is stealing as surely as robbing a bank is. Dishonest business dealings fall into this category. Ephesians 4:28 tells us, "Let him that stole steal no more: but rather let him labour, working with his hands the thing which is good, that he may have to give to him that needeth." Regardless of how valuable the item or how worthless, taking what is not ours is stealing.

> [9.] Thou shalt not bear false witness against thy neighbour.
>
> —Exodus 20:16

We are to be the bearers of truth and light, not untruths against others. If we give a testimony that is not true or repeat lies we have heard, we can do severe damage to the reputation of someone. We are not to heed lies against our neighbor or tell lies against them. Lying, according to the Scriptures, is a serious offense. "But the fearful, and unbelieving, and the abominable, and murderers, and whoremongers, and sorcerers, and idolaters, and *all liars*, shall have their part in the lake which burneth with fire and brimstone: which is the second death" (Rev. 21:8, emphasis added). Notice the word *liars* in that list. Also, in Revelation 21:27 in speaking of the city of God we read, "And there shall in no wise enter into it any thing that defileth, neither whatsoever worketh abomination, or *maketh a lie*: but they which are written in the Lamb's book of life" (emphasis added). Making a lie is deception.

To make something sound like or look like one thing when we know it is really something else is to make a lie, to deceive. It is wrong. God isn't just truthful, He *is* truth. Jesus said, "I am the way, the truth, and the life: no man cometh unto the Father, but my me" (John 14:6). We cannot reach the right destination without travelling the right way—the way of truth. When we join ourselves to a lie, we separate from Jesus, the Truth. Satan is the father of lies, and we have no business bearing a resemblance to him—no matter how innocent it may seem.

> [10.] Thou shalt not covet thy neighbour's house, thou shalt not covet thy neighbour's wife, nor his manservant, nor his maidservant, nor his ox, nor his ass, nor any thing that is thy neighbour's.
> —Exodus 20:17

To covet someone else's belongings is to desire something that does not belong to us. That is lust, a longing for something that is forbidden. Covetousness can lead to other sins, but it is a sin on its own. If we covet, we have an unthankful heart for the blessings of God in our life as we look longingly at what another person has. It also shows a lack of trust in God to provide us with all we need and what is best for us. Covetousness can lead to stealing, lying, murder, adultery, and other sins.

When Jesus was asked what the great commandment was He replied like this: "Thou shalt love the Lord thy God with all thy heart, and with all thy soul, and with all thy mind. This is the first and great commandment. And the second is like unto it, Thou shalt love thy neighbour as thyself. On these two commandments hang all the law and the prophets" (Matt. 22:37–40). God is first. His purposes come before any person, but people come next. Things are just tools to be used for God's purposes.

The Law had its weaknesses in that it was impossible for people to keep it all. If they failed in one aspect of the Law, they had failed completely. There was no hope; therefore, the blood of animal sacrifices was required to atone for our sins. God set up specific sacrifices to atone for the various sins, but they were only temporary and had to be repeated over and over. The yearly sacrifice was to rid the people of their sins as a whole, but it had to be made every year.

Yet the Law served the purpose God intended for it. The Law was the voice of God making His order known to a sinful people. It has shown us what sin is and the standard God has set before us. Imagine if everyone obeyed the Law of God fully. There would be no sin, no consequences of sin, no evil deeds, no innocent lives being lost, no wars, but peace. That is to come for those who have received the fulfillment of this Law—Jesus Christ. Although the Law points an accusing finger at our sins and shows us we are unable in ourselves to keep it, there is another step in God's order—full redemption.

chapter 7

Redemption

JESUS SAID, "FOR God sent not his Son into the world to condemn the world; but that the world through him might be saved" (John 3:17). How did Jesus bring about our redemption? It is in Jesus that "we have redemption through his blood, the forgiveness of sins, according to the riches of his grace" (Eph. 1:7).

What does it mean to redeem someone or something? It means to buy it back. When my son was three years old, I decided to sell some of his old toys that he did not play with anymore. At the family yard sale, he immediately identified a yellow, fuzzy pig as his own. He told my mother, "I wondered what happened to my pig. Do you have any money?" It broke my heart to find out he was going to buy back his prized possession. I did not realize he ever paid it any attention. It was returned to him at no cost, of course!

That is a wonderful example of our redemption. God had created mankind in a state of perfection and innocence with the absence of any evil to cause pain, death, or any troubles. He placed him in a perfect environment and had fellowship with him. When sin entered by the will of Adam and Eve, all the things God had protected them from came upon them. They were separated from Him because of their sin. They could no longer fellowship freely with God because of the wall of sin between them. God could have disowned them and given up the whole human race to destruction. But He didn't! Because of His love for us, He had already made provisions for cleansing from sin and a way back to fellowship with the Father. Even in the Garden of Eden He made mention of this salvation (Gen. 3:15). He made a way for us to reclaim our innocence and faultlessness. He made a way for the spirit that died to be resurrected in those who would receive His offer. Our bodies will die because of the curse, but our soul does not have to experience eternal damnation because Jesus Christ has made atonement for us.

My son did not have to pay to redeem his toy, but God paid a tremendous price for you and me. Yet He considered us worth the price. "For God so loved the world, that he gave his only begotten Son, that whosoever believeth in him should not perish, but have everlasting life" (John 3:16). Let us never take our redemption for granted, for the price was high, and only One was worthy enough to pay. It took a God-man to make the sacrifice, so Jesus was born of the Holy Spirit and of the Virgin Mary. He had no earthly father, but an earthly mother. His Father is God, and Jesus was very God and very man. He left the wonderful glories of Heaven to come to Earth and live a lifetime of being misunderstood, tempted, and mistreated to the climax of cruel crucifixion. Yet, He went through it all and died in our place so we could be free. If Jesus had been unwilling, we would be eternally lost in our sins.

Adam's sin caused every person after him to be born with a sin nature—the capability of committing every kind of evil. Before that time, humans carried the seed of goodness. After that time, they also carried the seed of evil. The seed bore fruit. It was sin. The Law was given to show the sin for what it was. Sin brought death. The Law required that blood be shed for our lawlessness. Redemption for our sins required death, our death. In order to keep us from eternal death, we needed a substitute. For years animal substitutes were used, but they were not able to remove the sin nature. Their blood covered sins only for a season. That is why the sacrifices had to be repeated again and again; even so, the heart remained unchanged.

The sacrifice Jesus made was necessary only once, not like the animal sacrifices offered by the people. He is our High Priest as well as the Lamb who was slain. Before His atonement, earthly men offered sacrifices of animals that were not exactly willing to be killed. But Jesus was the High Priest who offered Himself on the cross, shedding His blood for the remission of our sins once and for all.

> For such an high priest became us, who is holy, harmless, undefiled, separate from sinners, and made higher than the heavens; who needeth not daily, as those high priests, to offer up sacrifice, first for his own sins, and then for the people's: for this he did once, when he offered up himself.
> —HEBREWS 7:26–27

And so grace appeared. "For the law was given by Moses, but grace and truth came by Jesus Christ" (John 1:17). Grace is the divine touch of God on us and the enabling to work it out in our lives. Grace brings us back to God's order. It is then the Spirit of God will work in us and through us to touch other lives. Jesus came and brought this grace to everyone who will receive Him. He did this by His death on the cross, the shedding of His innocent blood. He was the sinless, spotless sacrifice required by God. Every sacrifice before Him had to be physically spotless and without blemish. There was not a human being who was not tainted with the essence of sin. Jesus was the only One who could live a perfect life and become that sacrifice, and He loved us enough to be willing to endure it all for us. Eternal life is ours simply by accepting the sacrifice of Jesus and being washed in His blood. Then we can bear the seed of the Spirit of God that produces eternal life rather than the seed of sin that produces ultimate death.

What is our part in this redemption process? We must believe—be totally convinced that God is true and rely completely on Christ for salvation, continuing in that confession. We must accept His sacrifice in our place "through faith in his blood" (Rom. 3:25).

Jesus is the mediator between God and us. Jesus bridged the gap spanning the giant chasm of sin that separates us from God. But we must walk across that bridge. There is only one Mediator. He is the only way to the Father.

Jesus came to accomplish certain purposes, and He

was completely successful. On the cross He said, "It is finished" (John 19:30).

He came to save sinners. "For the Son of man is come to seek and to save that which was lost" (Luke 19:10). After Satan caused the Fall and the sin nature became a part of every human, God came looking for us, just as He came looking for Adam and Eve. He knew what had happened, yet He sought them out to deal with the situation and make a way to draw them back to fellowship with Him. Jesus loved us first: "We love him, because he first loved us" (1 John 4:19). If God had not sent forth the call to us, we would be yet in our sins and without hope. There is nothing we can do within ourselves to rid us of sin. There is nothing we can do to rid ourselves of the barrier between us and God, but Jesus made a way. He sought us out and came to rescue us from our hopeless situation. He died for our sins in our place so we can have eternal life.

Jesus came to give life. "The thief cometh not, but for to steal, and to kill, and to destroy: I am come that they might have life, and that they might have it more abundantly" (John 10:10). The thieves Jesus refers to here are the hirelings or false ones who had come before Him. They did not do the works of the Father, but the works of the enemy. They were not sent from God but by Satan. Although Satan comes to steal our blessing, kill our souls, and destroy us, Jesus came to give us life that exceeds anything we have ever known. He came to give us eternal life.

Jesus came to destroy the works of the devil. "Forasmuch then as the children are partakers of flesh and blood, he also himself likewise took part of the same; that through death he might destroy him that had the power of death, that is, the devil: And deliver them who through fear of death were all their lifetime subject to bondage" (Heb. 2:14–15). In order to free us from sin, death, Hell, fear, and all the other devices of the devil, Jesus came and destroyed those works. We are still in this world, where those works are evident, but they do not have to be evident in us. We can be free! "He that committeth sin is of the devil; for the devil sinneth from the beginning. For this purpose the Son of God was manifested, that he might destroy the works of the devil" (1 John 3:8). We do not have to be in bondage to sin any longer. We have been given power over the works of the devil. "And he [Jesus] said unto them, I beheld Satan as lightning fall from heaven. Behold, I give unto you power to tread on serpents and scorpions, and over all the power of the enemy: and nothing shall by any means hurt you" (Luke 10:18–19). In the name of Jesus we have the power over the enemy. Instead of living lives of defeat doomed to destruction, we can live lives of holiness, righteousness, and power with the assurance of life eternal.

Jesus came to fulfill the Old Testament (or covenant). He did not do away with the Law. "Wherefore the law was our schoolmaster to bring us unto Christ, that we might be justified by faith" (Gal. 3:24). Since grace and truth came by Jesus Christ and grace is the touch of God on us and its outworking in our lives, the Law is now kept by the Spirit of God within us as we surrender to His leadership. Jesus said, "Think not that I am come to destroy the law, or the prophets: I am not come to destroy, but to fulfil. For verily I say unto you, Till heaven and earth pass, one jot or one tittle shall in no wise pass from the law, till all be fulfilled" (Matt. 5:17–18). Jesus fulfilled the natural by the spiritual. Through Jesus, the divine manifestation of God's order is completed. "God, who at sundry times and in divers manners spake in time past unto the fathers by the prophets, hath in these last days spoken unto us by his Son, whom he hath appointed heir of all things, by whom also he made the worlds" (Heb. 1:1–2). From Creation to the new Heaven and Earth, Jesus has been there. He always has been and always will be.

Jesus came to make it possible for us to enter the kingdom of God. This kingdom is a spiritual kingdom and an everlasting kingdom. (That is dealt with in another chapter.)

Jesus' death and resurrection rescued us from sin. But all of the human race is not automatically born again because Jesus died and rose again. We must realize that we are born sinners and, because we are sinners by nature, we commit any number of specific sins. "If we say that we have no sin, we deceive ourselves, and the truth is not in us. If we confess our sins, he is faithful and just to forgive us our sins, and to cleanse us from all unrighteousness. If we say that we have not sinned, we make him a liar, and his word is not in us" (1 John 1:8–10). We cannot save ourselves. We need a Savior. We must face the truth and agree with God about our sinful state before anything can be done about it. Once we have confessed our sinful condition, we can ask for forgiveness and receive a full pardon for every sin we have committed as well as having that old sin nature we were born with cut away. There is no other way to salvation except through Jesus. Jesus said, "I am the way, the truth, and the life: no man cometh unto the Father, but by me" (John 14:6). In Acts 4:12, Peter was speaking of Jesus Christ of Nazareth when he said, "Neither is there salvation in any other: for there is none other name under heaven given among men, whereby we must be saved."

"Therefore if any man be in Christ, he is a new creature: old things are passed away; behold, all things are become new" (2 Cor. 5:17). We are now free to walk in the Spirit. When Jesus ascended back into Heaven, the Holy Spirit of God came to dwell among those who become new creatures. Whereas Jesus in the flesh could only be at one place at a time, His Spirit could be within every believer at all times. Jesus had already told His disciples of the coming of His Spirit to dwell in them. (See Romans 8:11 and 1 Corinthians 3:16.) "But the Comforter, which is the Holy Ghost, whom the Father will send in my name, he shall teach you all things, and bring all things to your remembrance, whatsoever I have said unto you" (John 14:26). The Spirit of God dwells in us, teaching us, guiding us, comforting, and encouraging us. As Christ's new creation we must learn to yield to the Spirit of God within us and not our natural abilities.

We cannot be justified by the works of the Law. We

need more. We need that inward change that Jesus alone can give us. Paul puts it this way in Galatians 2:20: "I am crucified with Christ: nevertheless I live; yet not I, but Christ liveth in me: and the life which I now live in the flesh I live by the faith of the Son of God, who loved me, and gave himself for me."

> For in that he [Christ] died, he died unto sin once: but in that he liveth, he liveth unto God. Likewise reckon ye also yourselves to be dead indeed unto sin, but alive unto God through Jesus Christ our Lord. Let not sin therefore reign in your mortal body, that ye should obey it in the lusts thereof. Neither yield ye your members as instruments of unrighteousness unto sin: but yield yourselves unto God, as those that are alive from the dead, and your members as instruments of righteousness unto God. For sin shall not have dominion over you: for ye are not under the law, but under grace.
>
> —ROMANS 6:10–14

Now that the Spirit of God is within us, we must yield to Him. Our natural tendencies will draw us into sin if we allow them to, but we have the Spirit of God to show us a better way. It is a matter of yielding our thoughts and bodies to do what the Spirit prompts us to do and what the Bible tells us is right. "Know ye not, that to whom ye yield yourselves servants to obey, his servants ye are to whom ye obey; whether of sin unto death, or of obedience unto righteousness?" (Rom. 6:16). We either serve God or sin. The choice is ours.

Salvation from sin is not a one-time prayer that makes you feel a little better or joining a church and continuing on with life as it was. We are saved to begin a whole new life. Jesus becomes the center of everything else we do. He is the hub from which all the spokes extend.

> For by grace are ye saved through faith; and that not of yourselves: it is the gift of God: Not of works, lest any man should boast. For we are his workmanship, created in Christ Jesus unto good works, which God hath before ordained that we should walk in them.
>
> —Ephesians 2:8–10

We were condemned sinners before Jesus came. We could not save ourselves and sin reigned freely within us. When we become new creatures in Christ Jesus, our heart (the core or center of our existence) changes. Because of that change in who we are, what we do will change, too. Good works will flow from a pure heart, just as surely as evil works flow from an evil heart. God's Spirit within us will bear His fruit. "But the fruit of the Spirit is love, joy, peace, longsuffering, gentleness, goodness, faith, meekness, temperance: against such there is no law" (Gal. 5:22–23). The works or fruit of our old sin nature (the flesh) are listed in Galatians 5 as well: "Now the works of the flesh are manifest, which are these; Adultery, fornication, uncleanness, lasciviousness, Idolatry, witchcraft, hatred, variance, emulations, wrath, strife, seditions, heresies, Envyings murders, drunkenness, revellings, and such like: of the which I tell you before, as I have also told you in time past, that they which do such things shall not inherit the kingdom of God" (vv. 19–21). The good works found in the life of a believer are simply the results of a changed heart. The works are not the basis of our salvation, just the outworking. We cannot take credit for our salvation because we were completely powerless to change ourselves or our condition.

So, does this mean we will never sin again? No. But when we do sin, the Spirit of God will convict our hearts and draw us to immediate repentance. We must learn to yield, for there is cleansing from sin if we confess and repent. "My little children, these things write I unto you, that ye sin not. And if any man sin, we have an advocate with the Father, Jesus Christ the righteous: and he is the propitiation for our sins: and not for ours only, but also for the sins of the whole world" (1 John 2:1–2). The more we grow in Christ and yield to the leading of the Holy Spirit, the less we will sin. Sin will no longer be a common occurrence in our lives.

The sin nature that was born in mankind in the Garden of Eden causes us to live outside of God's order. It causes the plants and animals to live outside of God's created order; therefore, there is the need for redemption. We need to be cleansed from our sins, have the sin nature cut away, and have the Holy Spirit living within us. That restores the order of God in our lives in our spirit person. When we walk in the Spirit and cease to fulfill the lusts of the flesh (the longing for things that are forbidden), we will find ourselves going against the tide of this world system. That is why we were given the scripture in 2 Timothy 3:12, "Yea, and all that will live godly in Christ Jesus shall suffer persecution."

Everyone wants to know Jesus Christ. They just don't know what the longing in them is. They don't know their hunger is for the Holy Spirit and the Truth. Everyone is seeking the way to success, but only those who follow Jesus—the Way, the Truth, and the Life—ever find success. People seek fulfillment. There is only one way to be fulfilled, and that is to accept the blood of Jesus Christ as our atonement and to follow Him completely.

chapter 8

The Kingdom of God

DIMENSION IS THE limit that the mind can comprehend and the scope or extent of our actions and observations. It is the range in which we can be included. Our world is three-dimensional. We operate in movements that go up and down, right and left, and have depth. We are well acquainted with these dimensions. Our mind understands them. We are born into a world characterized by these three dimensions, and our actions and observations are contained within them. These three dimensions are the natural setting that define and control our boundaries. Our bodies are limited by these dimensions.

There are numerous scientific theories of other dimensions greater than our mind can conceive. We are not familiar with them because we are not included in them, cannot see them, and have no movement or knowledge in our 3-D world that is like them. Much study has been done on these dimensions. One report I read declared there was another dimension that moved in ways we cannot. They said it was the fourth dimension. However, I read another report that claimed the fourth dimension was time. Yet another report said there are possibly up to twenty-six dimensions we have not yet tapped into. All of this sounds like science fiction, and I don't have a clue what these scientists are talking about.

There is, however, a spiritual dimension that I do know about. It is called the kingdom of God. Jesus said in Luke 17:20–21, "The kingdom of God cometh not with observation: neither shall they say, Lo here! or, lo there! for, behold, the kingdom of God is within you." The kingdom of God cannot be seen with the natural eye. There is no ocular evidence that it exists. Those who are not born again of the Spirit of God cannot enter in because they cannot see it. Their mind cannot grasp it. Their extent of action, observation, and inclusion in this realm is nil. So how can we enter into this kingdom? The same way we entered this 3-D world—we are born into it!

John 3 contains the account of Jesus' conversation with Nicodemus, who was a learned man, a leader of the Jews, a Pharisee. He had obviously heard Jesus speak and had seen the miracles He had performed. He made this statement to Jesus: "Rabbi, we know that thou art a teacher come from God: for no man can do these miracles that thou doest, except God be with him" (John 3:2). Nicodemus was seeing and hearing things that were on a higher level than he was accustomed to. He watched a healing, but there was nothing for the eye to see except the sickness turned instantly to health. The natural healing we experience in this world is through a process that can be watched with the eye. A cut can be stitched back together.

Surgery can be done to remove tumors or diseased tissue. These processes can be observed, but the healings Jesus performed were not on this level. They were instantaneous and without any perceivable procedure. The words Jesus spoke were not dead words but words that came alive in Nicodemus' mind and heart. Something was different here than the lifeless religious rituals he had been going through all his life.

Jesus replied, "Verily, verily, I say unto thee, Except a man be born again, he cannot see the kingdom of God" (John 3:3). He went on to explain that unless a person is born physically *and* spiritually, they cannot enter into the kingdom of God. We cannot comprehend and be included in that realm until we are born into it. "That which is born of the flesh is flesh; and that which is born of the Spirit is spirit" (v. 6).

We are all born in the flesh with a body. The flesh is our physical being as well as our human nature. But human nature is carnal (having a darkened mind and living on a lower level of life). If we are to enter into a new dimension of life, we must be born into it by the Spirit of God. When we are born of the Spirit, we become enlightened to things above human comprehension and begin to live in a higher realm or kingdom than our body can allow us. Jesus is the only Way into that kingdom.

I was saved, or born again, when I was eleven years old. Nobody had to tell me something major had taken place. I was brand new, and I felt it. I had a sense of being and an awareness of the wonder of God's Spirit that I had not possessed before. Why? Because I had entered a higher dimension of life than I had known before. My spiritual eyes had been opened to the realm of God's kingdom. It felt that a part of me had awakened with a tingling excitement of new life. If you are born again, you have had the same experience, the same change, just under different physical circumstances.

Suddenly I was hungry to know Jesus personally, as well as His Word. Being born again transformed me from the inside out. My desires changed from temporal things to the eternal. Although I was very young, I wanted to spend time with Jesus and to learn His Word. "Therefore if any man be in Christ, he is a new creature: old things are passed away; behold, all things are become new" (2 Cor. 5:17). If there has been no change and no awakening to things of God's Spirit, there has been no new birth.

The process of being born again is not something we can do ourselves. It is a spiritual newness that comes only by the Holy Spirit. If we try to mentally learn the principles of the kingdom of God and intertwine them as best we can into our lives as we know it, we will be disillusioned with God and His principles. They are not designed to *work* on a natural level. We cannot bring God down to our level; we must move up to the new level He invites us to experience and inhabit. Mentally and physically trying to incorporate His standards on an earthly level will be completely frustrating, because the things of God are observed only on a spiritual level, not mentally. A genius without the Spirit of God cannot begin to understand what a person with a very low IQ with the Spirit of God can comprehend and operate in freely.

Many try to enter the world of the supernatural through various means. It is dangerous; in fact, it is deadly to do so any other way than through the blood of Jesus Christ shed for the remission of our sins. When they open themselves up in that way, their eyes are blinded further by the prince of darkness. He is the same one who promised Eve her eyes would be opened and she and Adam would be as gods if they would disobey God and eat the forbidden fruit. Satan lied to her, just like he lies to us today. Where she had been enlightened spiritually, darkness came, and her spiritual awareness was toward evil rather than good. Satan's "enlightenment" is always darkness that will destroy us. Rather than raising us to a new dimension, he delivers us to the pit of Hell. His promises of enlightenment sound grand, but he does not have that power, nor does he desire to reveal truth to mankind. He only wants to ensnare us. Many have traveled the path Satan offers, only to end up in eternal darkness and chains.

The Spirit of God is liberty, and the kingdom of God is righteousness, peace, and joy. You cannot find that in the devil's camp. Mankind is often curious about other-worldly phenomena and tries to enter the wrong way. Enlightenment is promised through New Age rhetoric and many religions; but there is only one way to God, and that is through Jesus Christ. Jesus said, "I am the way, the truth, and the life: no man cometh unto the Father, but by me" (John 14:6).

We must come through Jesus and be infused with the Spirit of God to make us aware of the things of His Spirit. Paul speaks about the hidden wisdom of God among those who are perfect (complete, mature in the Spirit):

> Eye hath not seen, nor ear heard, *neither have entered into the heart of man*, the things which God hath prepared for them that love him. *But God hath revealed them unto us by his Spirit....* Now we have received, not the spirit of the world, but the spirit which is of God; that we might know the things that are freely given to us of God. Which things also we speak, not in the words which man's wisdom teacheth, but which the Holy Ghost teacheth; comparing spiritual things with spiritual. But the natural man receiveth not the things of the Spirit of God: for they are foolishness unto him: neither can he know them, because they are spiritually discerned.
> —1 Corinthians 2:9–10, 12–14, emphasis added

Adam and Eve traded in the Spirit of God for the spirit of the world. They became natural. Because of their choice, we begin as natural—possessing only human nature rather than the nature of God—but we can be born a second time, this time into the dimension and realm of the kingdom of God. As born-again believers, we need to recognize our place and live up to the resources made available to us by the Spirit and the Word. The Spirit of God within us will teach us the meaning of the Word of

God like we could never comprehend before. As we read, He will illuminate our minds to understand the life of the Word of God—that same life that Nicodemus witnessed in the works of Jesus and in His teaching.

The kingdom of God cannot be seen with the natural eye but can be seen clearly with the spiritual eye. Those things that are hidden to the natural man are revealed to those who have received the Spirit. "It is the glory of God to conceal a thing: but the honour of kings is to search out a matter" (Prov. 25:2). We (those who are born again) are named kings and priests in Revelation 1:5–6. There is a spiritual level that we can observe, live in, have understanding of, and be included in now.

When I was in my early teens, I heard a preacher say that if our eyes were to be opened, we would see the room filled with spirits—angels and demons. The story of Elisha and his servant in 2 Kings 6 lets us see the reality of the spiritual activity that goes on around us.

The king of Syria felt threatened by Elisha the prophet, so he sent horses, chariots, and a great host to bring Elisha to him. Elisha's servant was frantic and said, "Alas, my master! how shall we do? And he answered, Fear not: for they that be with us are more than they that be with them. And Elisha prayed, and said, LORD, I pray thee, open his eyes, that he may see. And the LORD opened the eyes of the young man; and he saw: and, behold, the mountain was full of horses and chariots of fire round about Elisha" (2 Kings. 6:15–17). Elisha did not say, "They that be with us are more than they that be with them," as a motivational speech. He said it as a literal fact. God's angelic army was in array and ready to protect the man of God. They were there all the time in a dimension the young servant could not see. Obviously, Elisha saw them, but his servant could not see through spiritual eyes until Elisha asked God to open his eyes.

The eyes of the apostle Paul were opened to a higher dimension, which he referred to as the third Heaven. He mentions twice, "Whether in the body, or out of the body, I cannot tell: God knoweth" (2 Cor. 12:2–3). When he was there, he "heard unspeakable words, which it is not lawful for a man to utter" (v. 4). The manifest glory of God was too awesome to put into words. What he experienced was in a higher dimension than could be explained to the natural man.

Remember the donkey that Balaam rode? That donkey was allowed to glimpse into a higher realm. Three times he saw an angel poised to kill Balaam. Balaam's eyes were closed to the angel standing right in front of him until the Lord opened the mouth of the donkey to speak to Balaam. After that, "the LORD opened the eyes of Balaam, and he saw the angel of the LORD standing in the way, and his sword drawn in his hand: and he bowed down his head, and fell flat on his face" (Num. 22:31).

There are numerous accounts of angels being sent to give messages to people—Mary, Zacharias, Gideon, Daniel, the shepherds, and the list goes on. Ezekiel saw living creatures that could move in ways he could not comprehend. "And the living creatures ran and returned as the appearance of a flash of lightning" (Ezek. 1:14). He explains the motions of these creatures again in Ezekiel 10:11: "When they went, they went upon their four sides; they turned not as they went, but to the place whither the head looked they followed it; they turned not as they went."

Peter, James, and John saw in a new dimension on the Mount of Transfiguration. At that time, Jesus "was transfigured before them: and his face did shine as the sun, and his raiment was white as the light. And, behold, there appeared unto them Moses and Elias talking with him" (Matt. 17:2–3). Peter was ready to set up camp and stay in that dimension, but the time was not yet. There was work to do, and they had to go back off the Mountain of Transfiguration and get it done.

As children of God, we are aware of a higher dimension than those in the natural. We may not all be caught up into the third Heaven like Paul or have our eyes open to see the Lord's angels protecting us, but we can be aware of a greater dimension than this world. For every answer to prayer, there is spiritual activity that brought it about. When we experience great persecution or temptation, it is because of the evil spirits operating in a realm we cannot see. We see the people the evil spirits use, but God tells us we do not fight against flesh and blood "but against principalities, against powers, against the rulers of the darkness of this world, against spiritual wickedness in high places" (Eph. 6:12). If we are going to fight against evil spirits, we need the Holy Spirit to give us discernment and the power to overcome. That is why the armor of God is so important to us. It is a spiritual armor of protection and the sword of the Spirit (Word of God) for aggression. When we narrowly avoid an accident, spiritual circumstances have played a part.

When we become aware of this spiritual realm, our understanding in prayer, Bible reading, and life experiences become clearer. The Spirit of Christ will indwell us, and we begin to live in a heavenly kingdom even here on this Earth. But this world does not understand or desire the laws of the kingdom of God, so we find ourselves misunderstood, rejected, and, sometimes, persecuted.

Once we are born into the kingdom of God, we can grow from glory to glory. Paul speaks of the veil that has hidden the true, deeper meaning of the Law and blinded the eyes of those who do not receive Jesus and enter the kingdom of God: "Nevertheless when it [the heart of those who are blinded] shall turn to the Lord, the vail shall be taken away" (2 Cor. 3:16). Second Corinthians 3:18 in the Amplified Bible reads, "And all of us, as with unveiled face, [because we] continued to behold [in the Word of God] as in a mirror the glory of the Lord, are constantly being transfigured into His *very own* image in ever increasing splendor *and* from one degree of glory to another; [for this comes] from the Lord [Who is] the Spirit" (emphasis added). *Glory* refers to the manifest presence of God. His presence, nature, character, power, majesty, holiness, and authority become clear to us and are formed within us by His Spirit. We can have spiritual things revealed to us and shine out of us as lights to reveal Christ to the world.

As we grow more into the image of Jesus Christ by the Spirit of God at work in us, the things of this world grow dimmer and dimmer. Our priorities change. Our desires change. Our temperament and character change. Our lifestyle and thoughts change. We put aside all the "hidden things of darkness" (1 Cor 4:5), not because it is our duty but because we have had revealed to us the hidden "wisdom of God" (v. 7). Suddenly our range of inclusion expands to take in the spiritual realm.

> If then you have been raised with Christ [to a new life, thus sharing His resurrection from the dead], aim at and seek the [rich, eternal treasures] that are above, where Christ is, seated at the right hand of God. And set your minds and keep them set on what is above (the higher things), not on the things that are on the earth.
> —COLOSSIANS 3:1–2, AMP

Our new life raises us up above the common and the unclean—above the everydayness of this life and the wickedness that prevails in the world. The same invitation to come up is sent to every person on Earth. Only a few accept the invitation. Then only a few out of those who accept live fully in the privileges in the kingdom. They continue to live according to the principles of the world rather than the principles of a new dimension. Jesus said, "No man, having put his hand to the plough, and looking back, is fit for the kingdom of God" (Luke 9:62). No man who is seriously plowing a field will look backward. No person who is serious about following Jesus will continue to look back at the world. They will look forward unto Jesus, the Author and Finisher of our faith. I have been told when you are plowing, in order to keep a straight line, you need to set your sight on something before you in the distance and go toward it. We need to look continually to Jesus. We must turn our affections and allegiances toward the kingdom of God, not toward this world. We cannot be double minded and be enlarged in the kingdom.

"This I say then, Walk in the Spirit, and ye shall not fulfil the lust of the flesh" (Gal. 5:16). To walk in the Spirit is to live there, to deport oneself in full agreement with the nature, character, and principles of the kingdom of God. When we are absorbed with Jesus Christ, our desires will be for His kingdom, not for the natural things of this world.

What dimension are you living in? Are you stuck in a three-dimensional vacuum? Or have you been born again into the living, vibrant, victorious kingdom of our God? "Now we have received, not the spirit of the world, but the spirit which is of God; that we might know the things that are freely given to us of God" (1 Cor. 2:12).

"But rather seek ye the kingdom of God; and all these things shall be added unto you. Fear not, little flock; for it is your Father's good pleasure to give you the kingdom" (Luke 12:31–32). "These things" are the food, clothing, and shelter we need to survive in this world. While we must work to eat and provide for our temporal needs, our foremost thought is to be of God's kingdom. The kingdom of God and the kingdom of this earth cannot coincide in our hearts. We must choose which one we will give ourselves to. There is a great war between the two, and the choice is ours as to which we will yield.

Come higher and higher with Christ. Be changed into His image, and grow from glory to glory—revelation to revelation!

When Pilate questioned Jesus about the charges against Him, Jesus told him, "My kingdom is not of this world: if my kingdom were of this world, then would my servants fight, that I should not be delivered to the Jews: but now is my kingdom not from hence" (John 18:36). Jesus' kingdom is on a much higher plane than this world. If He only came to deliver the Jews from Rome, it would be only for one group of people in one certain circumstance and at one time in history. Jesus' work is not exclusive to time, place, persons, etc. It is for all people of all times and every place—*forever*! We accept the consequence of the curse on this world and our bodies because we don't know anything else; but there is life on a superior level than we experience here. Our minds can be enlightened to things beyond our comprehension. The Spirit of God can enlighten our spirits even now to give us a glimpse of the world to come and the wisdom to live by the government of God's kingdom even in this world.

The hymn-writer must have had great insight and

longing to live fully in this new dimension when he wrote:

> I'm pressing on the upward way, New heights I'm
>   gaining every day;
> Still praying as I onward bound, "Lord plant my feet on
>   higher ground."
>
> My heart has no desire to stay where doubts arise and
>   fears dismay;
> Tho' some may dwell where these abound, My prayer,
>   my aim is higher ground.
>
> I want to live above the world, Tho' Satan's darts at me
>   are hurled;
> For faith has caught the joyful sound, The song of saints
>   on higher ground.
>
> I want to scale the utmost height and catch a gleam of
>   glory bright;
> But still I'll pray till Heav'n I've found, "Lord, lead me
>   on to higher ground."
>
> Lord, lift me up and let me stand, by faith, on Heaven's
>   table-land.
> A higher plane than I have found; Lord, plant my feet
>   on higher ground.

This spiritual kingdom, the kingdom of God, is a real kingdom, one that lasts eternally and that has a government. The King reigns supremely and is perfect in justice. He never makes a mistake. He governs by the same principles He set up from the beginning—God's perfect order. Just as there was oneness with God, truth, peace, and perfection in the Garden of Eden; God has re-established His kingdom on Earth. The problems come because most choose not to live in His kingdom. The curse of sin is rampant, and there is a terrible war between God's kingdom and Satan's kingdom. This world is the battleground, but the war is a spiritual one.

We enter the kingdom immediately when we are born again, yet only in spirit, until we pass from this world to the next. We are members of His wonderful kingdom, yet we still have this body and live in this world that is under the curse. But someday it will all return to God's perfect order, with the curse abolished forever. So, for now we must resist the forces of evil by drawing close to God and staying in perfect relation to Him.

The foundation for living in this kingdom can be found in Isaiah 9:6:

> For unto us a child is born, unto us a son is given: and the government shall be upon his shoulder: and his name shall be called Wonderful, Counsellor, The mighty God, The everlasting Father, The Prince of Peace.

This passage is a prophecy of Jesus' birth into the world as our Savior. The Child *was* born. The Son *was* given—even unto death. But the government *is* upon His shoulder and shall be forever. He has the authority to control and to rule everything. He created it all! His rule will last forever.

We fight a losing battle if we rebel against God's government. However, it is not always easy shifting the control of our lives off of us and onto His shoulder. Our ways, thoughts, and understanding are not the same as His; but, His ways are perfect. It takes a deliberate changing of our will to set our path according to what God says in His Word regardless of how the situation seems to us. It requires learning His truth and abandoning our own opinions. It requires a close walk with Jesus all day, every day. The description of Jesus that follows gives us a guide as to how to release the government of our lives from our shoulder to His in every area. This will help us be good citizens of the heavenly kingdom.

The "shoulder" refers to the place on the neck between the shoulders where burdens are borne. We were not designed to bear those burdens, but Jesus is. In Matthew 11:28–30, Jesus invites us to shift the governing factor from our shoulder to His. "Come unto me, all ye that labour and are heavy laden, and I will give you rest. Take my yoke upon you, and learn of me; for I am meek and lowly in heart: and ye shall find rest unto your souls. For my yoke is easy, and my burden is light." That invitation still stands today. We can release the burden we bear over to Jesus and let Him be the governing factor in our lives, in every area. As we explore each area of His domain, we will see how we can relinquish ourselves into His hands completely, one step at a time.

Wonderful

When we admire someone, we speak well of them. Some people are extraordinary, and we say so. Many times people will go to extremes to please those in high places or those who are rich and famous. But there is One who is truly wonderful, and that is Jesus. When Ezekiel caught a glimpse into Heaven, he saw the wonder of our God—the splendor and awe of the Almighty as He sat on the throne.

> And above the firmament that was over their heads was the likeness of a throne, as the appearance of a sapphire stone: and upon the likeness of the throne was the likeness as the appearance of a man above upon it. And I saw as the colour of amber, as the appearance of fire round about within it, from the appearance of his loins even upward, and from the appearance of his loins even downward, I saw as it were the appearance of fire, and it had brightness round about. As the appearance of the bow that is in the cloud in the day of rain, so was the appearance of the brightness round about. This was the appearance of the likeness of the glory of the Lord. And when I saw it, I fell upon my face, and I heard a voice of one that spake.
>
> —Ezekiel 1:26–28

John saw a very similar sight when he was on the Isle of Patmos. They saw the kingdom of God as it shall be for us when we are released from this body and this world.

John wrote:

> The four and twenty elders fall down before him
> that sat on the throne, and worship him that
> liveth for ever and ever, and cast their crowns
> before the throne, saying, Thou art worthy, O
> Lord, to receive glory and honour and power: for
> thou hast created all things, and for thy pleasure
> they are and were created.
>
> —Revelation 4:10–11

These crowns mentioned in Revelation are symbols of rewards received for works done, yet the elders cast them at Jesus' feet. Certainly we are called to good works, but not for the works' sake. Everything we do is to be done for the glory of God. Worship Jesus. Our position and accomplishments fade in the light of His presence. Too often our eyes are on other people as we compete against them. Our eyes need to be on the wonderful One and our hearts set on doing His will. It is an immense privilege to be able to know Jesus personally. He is the ruler of the universe. If you can think of the most important, influential, powerful person you know, be assured Jesus is in control of him. Take time with Him. Allow yourself to be drawn into His presence.

Counsellor

When we need advice, we should immediately think of Jesus. When we get off track, need to make a decision, or face impossible odds, Jesus is the answer. He can counsel us in every area of life. He has been tempted at all points as we have, yet He never sinned or made a mistake (Heb. 4:15). There is no better counselor than Jesus.

Mere human counselors, no matter how educated they are, cannot see the whole picture of our lives. They know only what we tell them and about general human nature. But we are not all made alike and do not fall into a "general human nature" category in every situation. I have had some very bad advice from well-meaning Christians. If I had followed it, I would have sustained serious damage to my life and been outside of God's will. The Lord knows all angles of our problems. He knows the past, present, and future. He knows our name, our motives, our hang-ups, and our hearts. We know we will get the truth when we seek God's resolution to every circumstance and that it will be on an individual basis. Those who only seek someone to agree with them rather than to know the truth can travel from counselor to counselor and finally find one that will tell them their opinion is right. But, if we want the truth, we will go to Jesus and His Word. Our opinions or the opinions of others should never take precedence over God's Word.

Once I heard the story of a hunter who set out to find a bear with one thought in mind—a fur coat. When he found a bear, things did not go as expected. As he raised his rifle to shoot, the bear began to speak. He said, "You don't really want to do that. Wait a minute, and let's come up with a compromise." The hunter was willing and said he wanted a fur coat. The bear said he knew the perfect compromise for them both to have what they wanted. A few minutes later the bear walked away alone, and they both had what they wanted. The hunter had a fur coat, and the bear had a full stomach. The hunter should have stood like a rock. This was no time to swim with the current.

If we consider the Word of God (His counsel) negotiable, the devil will work out a compromise just for us, but we always wind up the loser. Remember, he offered a deal to Eve in the Garden of Eden that sounded too good to be true, and it was. It was just what she wanted to hear and believe, but it cost too much in the end. What we believe does not change the truth, but it does determine our path in life and our destination when this life is over. Satan wants to reach a compromise with you in your situation today, but a compromise is too big a price to pay. He only comes to steal, kill, and destroy; yet, he makes it seem as if he is offering the fulfillment of our dreams. The Scriptures say he can come as an angel of light, but he is full of darkness and has no real light to give. His schemes always bring us ruin.

We can receive counsel in most of life's circumstances by going directly to the Bible. Other times the Lord will show us the way by the leading of His Spirit in our hearts. Yet, we must have a heart willing to listen and obey.

> I will instruct thee and teach thee in the way
> which thou shalt go: I will guide thee with mine
> eye. Be not as the horse, or as the mule, which
> have no understanding: whose mouth must be

held in with bit and bridle, lest they come near
unto thee.

—Psalm 32:8–9

If we yield ourselves to the Spirit of God, we will save
ourselves the pain of the bit and bridle. That requires
being attentive to His gentle nudgings. If we are stub-
born, we may have to experience hurt to learn the lessons
we need to take us in the direction the Lord is leading.
Our culture teaches us that to be totally independent of
anyone else is the main objective in life, but God's Word
teaches complete dependence on Him. Learn to seek out
the Counselor and obey Him.

Mighty God

Our God has all power. He is as mighty today as He
was when He spoke and created the world; when He rolled
back the Red Sea; when He made the walls of Jericho fall;
when He healed the sick, cast out demons, and raised the
dead.

We can look to Jesus to have our every need supplied. If
He did not want us to depend on Him, He would not tell
us of His might and invite us into His kingdom. When
we have a need, we are to take it immediately to the Lord
in prayer.

> Be careful [anxious] for nothing; but in every thing
> by prayer and supplication with thanksgiving let
> your requests be made known unto God…But

> my God shall supply all your need according to
> his riches in glory by Christ Jesus.
>
> —PHILIPPIANS 4:6, 19

Not only is God willing to supply our needs, He has the might and power to do it. Have you ever had a problem and knew no one could solve it, but it made you feel better to talk about it? That may solve the momentary emotions within us, but it does not change our circumstances. We need to take every problem, every decision to our mighty God and *expect* Him to do something about it. Prayer does make us feel better, but that is not the only result we can receive. God is a consoling God, and in His presence we can find peace; but He is also a mighty God who moves on our behalf. We need to pray in such a way that we expect to receive the answer.

Psalm 62:5 says, "My soul, wait thou only upon God; for my expectation is from him." To expect God to hear and answer in this passage indicates that the one waiting is doing so with outstretched neck. It reminds me of waiting for a parade to begin while in the midst of a crowd. People stand on tiptoe to see over the obstacles in their way and crane their necks to catch a glimpse of the beginning of the parade as it makes its way down the street. They know it's coming. They have no doubt whatsoever. It is just a matter of time.

When we pray with expectation, we begin to look over all the obstacles for the answer in full assurance that God has it on the way. He comes in power to change our situation, to change us. Sometimes we are the ones that need changing, not our circumstances.

We can receive counsel from the King of this heavenly kingdom *and* the power to follow that counsel to bring forth change in our lives. Expect our mighty God to move in your life.

Everlasting Father

This kingdom is also a family with a royal blood line. We must accept the blood of Jesus to cleanse us from sin before we become a part of this royal family.

Do we bear the family resemblance? When people see us, do they know we are related to Christ? Just as we have physical characteristics that link us with our earthly families, we should openly show the world we belong to Christ. Those of royal blood are meticulously instructed in etiquette, the "rules of the royal," even from infancy. We become very much like our earthly family members in our mannerisms, habits, character, and opinions; and this should also be true in the spiritual. People should sense that we belong to our heavenly Father and see the difference in us by our mannerisms, habits, character, and opinions. In other words, we are to walk worthy of the calling of Christ Jesus.

The father is the head of the family. He has been given that position by God and is the one who has the authority to make decisions for the family. Our everlasting Father has all authority in Heaven and Earth, and it will never, never, never end!

Eventually children grow up, have their own homes, and become the authority they once were under. This is not true in the kingdom of God. Our Father is everlastingly the Father and we are His children. We never outgrow His authority.

Psalm 27:10 says, "When my father and my mother forsake me, then the LORD will take me up." The word *forsake* means "to loosen or relinquish," not "to abandon or desert," as we would usually think. It is not normal for parents to forsake their children in that way, regardless of how old they become. They don't turn their backs on them, but are always there to advise and love them even when they are grown. However, they relinquish the control they had over their children when they were young. The children support themselves, make their own decisions, and raise their own families.

Psalm 71:9 shows God's authority and care go beyond childhood. It lasts forever. "Cast me not off in the time of old age; forsake me not when my strength faileth." He is the everlasting Father, ever in power.

Prince of Peace

Everyone wants peace—nations, churches, businesses, homes, individuals. Isaiah 26:3–4 tells us how to accomplish that: "Thou wilt keep him in perfect peace, whose mind is stayed on thee: because he trusteth in thee. Trust ye in the LORD for ever: for in the LORD JEHOVAH is everlasting strength." Our minds often stray to other means of gaining peace, but the Lord is our only Source of true peace. His kingdom is one of peace—at one with God and therefore at one with each other. If we attain the world's peace, it is momentary, fleeting; but Jesus said His peace was not like that. We need to fill our minds with Jesus, the Word. We should train ourselves to think the way God says to think. Just as we put off evil deeds and replace them with good deeds, we must replace carnal thoughts with God's Word. That involves relinquishing our will and using discipline along with the power of the Holy Spirit.

Colossians 3:15 tells us more about the peace of God: "And let the peace of God rule in your hearts, to the which also ye are called in one body; and be ye thankful." The word *rule* means "to act as an umpire." There are some things we plainly know are either right or wrong, but there are times when we don't know. When we must choose a job, a spouse, or which church to attend, we cannot know which will be the best for the future; but, God can. So in times like that, in those tough calls of life, we can let the peace of God act as an umpire. To have true peace is to be at one with God. If we begin to make the wrong decision, our spirit will let us know we are about to move outside of God's will (His order). It is often subtle, but if we listen, His peace will make the right call. Often we lose our peace and put ourselves in a position of confusion and turmoil when we try to handle situations on our own without considering the Lord.

When I was a little girl, I went to visit a friend of mine. She had a pony, and I was privileged to ride it. There was a problem, though. That pony had a mind of its own and a strong will. No sooner was I on its back than it decided to run—straight for a clothesline stretched across the back yard. During my ride, I could hear my friend's voice behind me frantically yelling, "Lie down!" I did lie down, just in time to keep from being seriously injured.

When we take off running on sheer will power, we will cause injury, whether to ourselves, someone else, or both. Confusion will reign when we exert our will over God's, and peace will elude us. Submitting to the will of God alone will bring us lasting peace. If we try to make choices by what *seems* best, we usually regret it. The Lord knows what *is* right, not just what *seems* right. Ruling our own lives will be more than we can bear if we try to carry that burden ourselves. We will be overwhelmed and see no way out. When your peace is interrupted, stop, take inventory, and ask God to show you where you have gone wrong. If we lose our peace, we are out of step with God in some area. It may be a small thing or a major issue. If we are in confusion, God is not controlling the situation; we are holding on to the reins and are out of control. He is "not the author of confusion, but of peace" (1 Cor. 14:33).

Remember, too that our intellect may not understand what God's Spirit is saying to us, but our spirit will when we are at one with Him. "And the peace of God, which passeth all understanding, shall keep your hearts and minds through Christ Jesus" (Phil. 4:7). Let Jesus be the Prince of Peace in every part of your life.

Isaiah 9:7 continues on about the government of His kingdom:

> Of the increase of his government and peace there shall be no end, upon the throne of David, and upon his kingdom, to order it, and to establish it with judgment and with justice from henceforth even for ever. The zeal of the LORD of hosts will perform this.

There is no doubt His kingdom will continue. It will increase—produce offspring and gain interest on capital. Since Jesus came there have been many born into the kingdom of God. His Word has increased in the world and will continue forever. His kingdom has been set up, strengthened, and supported by His miracles, might, counsel, peace, and perpetuity. It has been established with His divine law and virtue (that which is right and just). His zeal will bring it to pass just as He said. It is a sure thing.

If you had money to invest in stock and you found something that you knew without any doubt would be strong, increase as time continued, and its success would last forever, you would probably borrow more money to invest. You would put everything you had into that venture.

We know the surety of God's kingdom. It is strong and will increase forever. We would be wise to put everything we have and everything we are into His kingdom.

Allow His counsel to be the final authority in your life.

Don't lean on your own understanding. (See Proverbs 3:5.) It will only bring confusion. Don't be a disobedient child to your Father, but allow Him to gather you to Himself and show you the way. Don't strive for position; rather, strive to know Christ. When you need a counselor, seek God's Word. He may use other people to show you His Word, but make sure they are accurate. Always accept the advice of the Word of God. Turn the government of your life over to Him, because "of the increase of His government and peace there shall be no end.... The zeal of the LORD of hosts will perform this" (Isa. 9:7).

It is difficult to be from one country and live in another country. The culture and rules are all different, and we do not fit in. Those who are born again have been born into a spiritual kingdom, one that cannot be seen with the natural eye, but it is just as real as and more lasting than the flesh-and-blood world we live in now. The new kingdom embodies the spirit that was in the Garden of Eden.

Jesus preached the good news of the kingdom of God. "Now after that John was put in prison, Jesus came into Galilee, preaching the gospel of the kingdom of God, and saying, The time is fulfilled, and the kingdom of God is at hand: repent ye, and believe the gospel" (Mark 1:14–15). The Gospels in the Bible are filled with Jesus' teachings on the kingdom of God. Reread the four Gospels to gain more insight into His kingdom.

Jesus spoke of the kingdom of God or the kingdom of Heaven often. He spoke of it being at hand. His disciples believed it to be the emerging of a physical kingdom that would free them from Roman rule, but Jesus was speaking of the spiritual kingdom that begins in our hearts in this life and transports us into the fullness of His kingdom. That fulfillment comes when we shed the body that holds us down and leave behind the carnal system that prevents the kingdom of God from being fully workable in this world. The sin in the world and the resistance against God's order keep us from realizing His kingdom in its wholeness—its complete state. But the day is coming when we can live completely in the kingdom of God without any opposition from outward circumstances, people, or demonic activity.

As Christians, we have been commissioned to continue the work Jesus started. When He sent forth the disciples, He gave them these instructions: "And as ye go, preach, saying, The kingdom of heaven is at hand. Heal the sick, cleanse the lepers, raise the dead, cast out devils: freely ye have received, freely give" (Matt. 10:7–8). They were given power to carry out those instructions.

Just before Jesus ascended back to the Father, He gave them similar instructions:

> All power is given unto me in heaven and in earth. Go ye therefore, and teach all nations, baptizing them in the name of the Father, and of the Son, and of the Holy Ghost: Teaching them to observe all things whatsoever I have commanded you:

> and, lo, I am with you always, even unto the end of the world.
>
> —MATTHEW 28:18–20

The gospel message has been preached over most of the world. I don't know if those in absolutely every nook and cranny have heard yet, but they will. "And this gospel of the kingdom shall be preached in all the world for a witness unto all nations; and then shall the end come" (Matt. 24:14). The end of this world order is coming. Then the kingdom of God will be in its complete and full state. We will live in Heaven eternally with Jesus, where God's kingdom will continue without hindrance.

As Jesus prayed to His Father in Matthew 6:13: "For thine is the kingdom, and the power, and the glory, for ever. Amen."

chapter 9

The Church

THERE WAS A time when God said to build Him a tabernacle. He told Moses, "Speak unto the children of Israel, that they bring me an offering: of every man that giveth it willingly with his heart ye shall take my offering....And let them make me a sanctuary; that I may dwell among them" (Exod. 25:2, 8). Their offerings were to be the materials needed to build the tabernacle and furnish it. Note, also, they were to be given with willing hearts. That is the only offering God accepts. Many years after the tabernacle, a temple was built where God's presence was manifest.

We live under a new covenant now. He is not looking for a temple made with hands. Our bodies are the temple of the Holy Ghost—the presence of God in the earth.

> What? know ye not that your body is the temple of the Holy Ghost which is in you, which ye have of God, and ye are not your own? For ye are bought with a price: therefore glorify God in your body, and in your spirit, which are God's.
> —1 CORINTHIANS 6:19–20

In John 4: 21–24, Jesus prophesied of the day when His temple would no longer be in one place, but in our hearts.

Our offering given to prepare the temple is not to be material things, but all that we are. The sacrifice we offer up to God must be given willingly with our hearts. Romans 12:1 says, "I beseech you therefore, brethren, by the mercies of God, that ye present your bodies a living sacrifice, holy, acceptable unto God, which is your reasonable service." The presence of God dwells in His church, not the buildings we pay so much attention to but the collective body of believers in Jesus Christ. It is made up of individuals who will give themselves completely to the Lord. It is a spiritual building that will last forever.

THE CHURCH'S FOUNDATION

Toward the end of Jesus' earthly ministry, He asked the disciples who men were saying He was. They said, "Some say that thou art John the Baptist: some, Elias; and others, Jeremias, or one of the prophets" (Matt. 16:14). His next question was of major importance. He asked them—His closest followers, the ones He had poured Himself into:

> But whom say ye that I am? And Simon Peter answered and said, Thou art the Christ, the Son of the living God. And Jesus answered and said unto him, Blessed art thou, Simon Barjona: for flesh and blood hath not revealed it unto thee, but my Father which is in heaven. And I say also unto

thee, That thou art Peter, and upon this rock I will build my church; and the gates of hell shall not prevail against it. And I will give unto thee the keys of the kingdom of heaven: and whatsoever thou shalt bind on earth shall be bound in heaven: and whatsoever thou shalt loose on earth shall be loosed in heaven.

—MATTHEW 16:15–19

Jesus told Peter he was blessed, enlarged, and happy. He had taken a step beyond believing Jesus was a great man who would free them from Roman rule. The revelation of Jesus that Peter had was not given to him by a mere human being nor by his experiences in life. God, the Father Himself, had disclosed this to him. This was spiritual knowledge that superseded anything natural.

Jesus then began to continue a conversation He had with Peter at their first meeting when He said, "Thou art Simon the son of Jona: thou shalt be called Cephas, which is by interpretation, A stone" (John 1:42). The name Peter means "a piece of a rock, larger than a stone." Peter had certainly been enlarged since his first meeting with Jesus. He was obviously a strong man in the natural, but he would be stronger by this revelation and following where it would take him. Peter would play an important part in the establishing of the church. Jesus went on to say on this rock (a mass of rock, not just one part) He would construct His church. The foundation of the church is built on this revelation of Jesus as the Christ, the Son of the living God. Jesus Christ is the Cornerstone of the church. The apostles helped to lay the foundation as they spread the gospel by the power of the Holy Spirit.

> And ye are built upon the foundation of the apostles and prophets, Jesus Christ himself being the chief corner stone; In whom all the building fitly framed together groweth unto an holy temple in the Lord: In whom ye also are builded together for an habitation of God through the Spirit.
> —EPHESIANS 2:20–22

The cornerstone gives the building its strength and integrity. It brings it together with stability and security.

The church is not the foundation. Jesus is, but we are "lively stones" that make up the house of God.

> Ye also, as lively stones, are built up a spiritual house, an holy priesthood, to offer up spiritual sacrifices, acceptable to God by Jesus Christ. Wherefore also it is contained in the scripture, Behold, I lay in Sion a chief corner stone, elect, precious: and he that believeth on him shall not be confounded.
> —1 PETER 2:5–6

God is not in the market for a house made with human hands. He no longer chooses to make His presence known through a building or in a certain place, but through people—His people. He is building His temple in you and me—those who are called out of the world system and into the order He created for us. He is calling us out of the natural and into the spiritual kingdom that will last forever. This congregation is made up of every person from every generation who believes in the name of Jesus Christ. The church that Jesus is building will stand firm and secure. If you want to help build the church, begin to pour the Word of God into those around you. We do that by building one another up in the faith.

The very power and authority of death, Hell, and the grave cannot overpower God's church. The word *Hell* here means "Hades, the place of the dead;" but it also means "to be unseen." Something that is unseen is hidden from our eyes. It does not mean it does not exist. It is just the opposite of what had happened to Peter when the Father revealed the truth to him and opened his eyes to heavenly things. It is the opposite of awareness, understanding, and knowledge. The power of evil to deceive and delude us cannot overcome the Spirit of God who brings revelation knowledge to us. The light of Jesus Christ dispels the darkness and allows us to see spiritual things as they are.

Jesus told Peter He would give him the keys of the kingdom of Heaven. Keys are symbolic of authority. If you have a key to a building, you can either open the door for others to enter or lock it and shut them out. Jesus told the teachers of the Law they had taken away the key of knowledge so others could not enter the kingdom of Heaven: "Woe unto you, lawyers! for ye have taken away the key of knowledge: ye entered not in yourselves, and them that were entering in ye hindered [forbade or prevented]" (Luke 11:52).

The message Peter preached opened the doors to those who would believe in the name (character and authority) of Jesus Christ and closed the doors to those who would turn aside to find another way, for there is no other way. When the five wise virgins in Jesus' parable went to the wedding supper, they were allowed in. The five foolish virgins who had run out of oil were not allowed in. They were unfaithful and careless about their souls, and the door remained shut to them. (See Matthew 25:1–13.) With the authority to unlock the gospel message, Jesus' disciples would be foundational in the church.

We must remember this gospel was a brand new word from God. They were accustomed to the Law of Moses and the Prophets; and, although these prophesied of the Messiah, men's interpretations of His coming were inaccurate. The disciples were the first ones to be taught the gospel by Jesus and empowered to teach it and live it by the Holy Spirit. They began to preach it as Jesus had commanded them. From them, the message has been spread worldwide and for many generations. We take for granted the message because it was there before we were and we grew up with knowledge of the gospel. That was not the case for the first Christians. It is easy to forget how new this was to the whole world. Those who would believe entered the kingdom of God.

THE CHURCH'S EMPOWERMENT

In Luke 4:18, Jesus said, "The Spirit of the Lord is upon me, because he hath anointed me." We'll look at the rest of this passage later, but, before we can do what follows, we need the power to do it.

First, we need the Spirit of God. Without His Spirit, we cannot understand the mission or the message, nor can we share it effectively with others. In Acts 2, we read the account of the Holy Spirit being poured out on those in the Upper Room. These people were followers of Jesus when He was alive in the flesh. They believed Him enough to obey His command to wait for the promise of the Father. Jesus had told them, "Ye shall receive power, after that the Holy Ghost is come upon you: and ye shall be witnesses unto me both in Jerusalem, and in all Judaea, and in Samaria, and unto the uttermost part of the earth" (Acts 1:8).

What was the first thing the disciples did when they received the Holy Ghost? They began to speak in the tongues of all those gathered in Jerusalem for the Feast of Pentecost. What were they saying in these languages they had not learned? They spoke of "the wonderful works of God" (Acts 2:7). They immediately became endued with supernatural power to witness of the Lord Jehovah.

Everyone was perplexed because it was obvious these men were not learned men, yet they were speaking foreign languages fluently. "And they were all amazed, and were in doubt, saying one to another, What meaneth this?" (Acts 2:12). Peter began to explain beginning with the prophet Joel, who had prophesied of this event. He proceeded to speak of Jesus of Nazareth, whom they had murdered and whom God had raised from the dead. He backed up the message of Jesus with the history of King David. He ended with this: "Therefore let all the house of Israel know assuredly, that God hath made that same Jesus, whom ye have crucified, both Lord and Christ" (v. 36). When they were convicted in their hearts and asked what they could do, Peter gave them the answer. "Repent, and be baptized every one of you in the name of Jesus Christ for the remission of sins, and ye shall receive the gift of the Holy Ghost" (v. 38). Three thousand souls believed that day and became a part of the kingdom of God. All those who are born in to the kingdom of God are collectively called the church.

From that point on, the disciples began to continue the work that Jesus started. How could they do that? They had the anointing of the Holy Spirit. In Luke 4:18, Jesus spoke of His anointing. Once the Holy Spirit was poured out, those who believed in Jesus received that anointing. They were consecrated to Christ and His work. The Holy Spirit provided what they needed to *be* as well as to *do*. This provision comes from being in close contact with the person.

If I started a small business and you provided the capital by sending money, you would be helping to supply one of the needs. But if you came to the business with your money and business expertise and worked with me side-by-side daily to establish the company and develop the ongoing operation, you would have become a vital part of the business in an all-consuming way. This is how vitally connected we need to be with the Spirit of God. We are yoked together with God's Spirit to accomplish a common goal. Many people may be what we call church members, but they are not part of the kingdom of God. Attending church services does not mean we are born again. There are within our church organizations those who are truly part of God's church, but many are only active in organized religion.

Jesus spoke of how we should take His yoke upon us. That means to work side by side with Him, going the same direction with the same purpose at heart. We do not have to bear the whole burden alone. His Spirit is alongside us, providing guidance and strength for the job we need to do.

Jesus told His disciples the Holy Spirit was coming to be with them. He called Him the Comforter in John 14, 15, and 16. This, once again, has the meaning of calling someone to your side. The Comforter is here to lead us. If you can't find your way through a maze, it is a comfort to have someone call to you and say, "Stay close beside me, and I will get you through the maze." The Holy Spirit will do that if we will listen to His voice and stay close to Him. Jesus did this for His disciples in a bodily sense when He was among them. Yet, He told them it was advantageous to the disciples if He left them and sent the Holy Spirit in His place so we could be filled with the Holy Ghost. The gospel message was about to explode and encompass more people than Jesus could be with in the flesh, but in the Spirit He could be alongside each person.

The Holy Spirit was given to enlighten, enable, and

provide whatever we need to do the work of the kingdom. That is where it starts. Jesus was anointed. That anointing has been passed on to us—that enabling by contact with Him.

> But we have an unction [anointing] from the Holy One, and ye know all things....But the anointing which ye have received of him abideth in you, and ye need not that any man teach you: but as the same anointing teacheth you of all things, and is truth, and is no lie, and even as it hath taught you, ye shall abide in him.
>
> —1 JOHN 2:20, 27

God's Spirit has called us near to Him. It is up to us to answer the call and stay close by learning to walk in the Spirit.

THE CHURCH'S MISSION

Now that we know where the wisdom and ability to do the work comes from, what is the work? The mission of the church is to preach the gospel. So, what is the gospel? It is God's systematic plan for our total redemption. Jesus' teachings, His works, His lifestyle, His character, and everything He showed us are a part of the gospel message. His mission is our mission. Jesus gave us the power we need to accomplish His mission as well as insight into the nature of our mission when He made His proclamation in Luke 4:18–19:

> The Spirit of the Lord is upon me, because he
> hath anointed me to preach the gospel to the
> poor; he hath sent me to heal the brokenhearted,
> to preach deliverance to the captives, and recov-
> ering of sight to the blind, to set at liberty them
> that are bruised, To preach the acceptable year of
> the Lord.

What has the Spirit come alongside to accomplish
through us? For what purpose has He given us ability and
authority? Let's go step by step and see. A parallel to the
passage in Luke 4 is Ezekiel 34:4. It gives us further insight
into the meaning of our mission. Although the passage is
from a negative point of view of the maltreatment of the
people by the spiritual leaders, it tells us what is expected
by the clear rebuke for what they have not done.

> The diseased have ye not strengthened, neither
> have ye healed that which was sick, neither have
> ye bound up that which was broken, neither have
> ye brought again that which was driven away,
> neither have ye sought that which was lost; but
> with force and with cruelty have ye ruled them.

Jesus is the Good Shepherd and leads and cares for His
sheep gently, yet firmly.

First, He has anointed us "to preach the gospel to the
poor" (Luke 4:19). Preaching the gospel is announcing the
good news. The Greek word that is translated "poor" in
this passage means "a public beggar." Many people may

lack the funds others have, but often this can be hidden from the eyes of other people. In this case, however, the poverty is such that it cannot be hidden. It is evident and common knowledge among the public. Spiritually, we are nothing more than public beggars asking for mercy that we do not deserve. That may seem to be a hopeless case except for the grace and mercy of God and the sacrifice of Jesus Christ to cleanse us completely from sin and make us fit to stand before God, clothed in His righteousness. Because of Jesus, we can be made children of the King of all kings. How can we keep such good news to ourselves?

When Jesus was born, these good tidings were announced by the angels:

> And the angel said unto them, Fear not: for, behold, I bring you good tidings of great joy, which shall be to all people. For unto you is born this day in the city of David a Saviour, which is Christ the Lord.... And suddenly there was with the angel a multitude of the heavenly host praising God, and saying, Glory to God in the highest, and on earth peace, good will toward men.
>
> —LUKE 2:10–11, 13–14

This baby was the Son of God and came to bring peace (being set at one with God) to the Earth. It was a message of good will, not judgment.

Now, it is our turn to announce these glad tidings! When Jesus told the disciples He was going to send the Holy Ghost to give them power, He also told them what they were to use that power for: "And ye shall be witnesses unto me both in Jerusalem, and in all Judea, and in Samaria, and unto the uttermost part of the earth" (Acts 1:8).

In Luke 24 Jesus speaks of preaching in His name among all nations: "Thus it is written, and thus it behooved Christ to suffer, and to rise from the dead the third day: And that repentance and remission of sins should be preached in his name among all nations, beginning at Jerusalem. And ye are witnesses of these things" (vv. 46–48). Who is responsible for proclaiming the gospel message? Those who are witnesses of Jesus Christ. If we are born again, we have the responsibility to make known the gospel message of Jesus' birth, life, death, and resurrection and the impact it has on us.

Those who are called as witnesses in a court of law are there to tell what they saw and heard first hand, with the purpose of helping the jury distinguish the truth. There are many who need us to tell them and show them the truth. They are looking for what is true—and the proof. Those who are lost need to know they have a Savior. The things Jesus shares with us, we need to pass along—the good news of our salvation and our new birth into the kingdom of God. "What I tell you in darkness, that speak ye in light: and what ye hear in the ear, that preach ye upon the housetops" (Matt. 10:27).

"He hath sent me to heal the brokenhearted" (Luke 4:19). To be sent is to be set apart for a particular mission. If you are born again, you have been set apart to tell people about Jesus, simply to give your eyewitness account and personal experience. Those who are brokenhearted have had the center of their being crushed, and only the touch of Jesus can make them whole again. He is the only One who can put all the pieces together and make it better than before. Once He has done it for us, we can share it with others.

In Ezekiel 34:4 we find the shepherd's job is to bind up the broken. When a bone is broken, a part of our support structure has been snapped. We can either leave it alone and be crippled, or we can have it reset and allow it to heal properly. There are many people around us whose support system is broken, and they need it to be set and wrapped tightly so it can be restored. They may need us to lend support while they undergo the healing process.

Because of Adam and Eve's sin, we are all born spiritually deficient and crippled. Some people have become brokenhearted because of something they have experienced in life. Jesus can reset our spirits and renew us. People need to hear that message from those who have received it firsthand.

"[He hath sent me] to preach deliverance to the captives" (Luke 4:19). The word *preach* in this passage means "to herald divine truth as a public crier would announce publicly the latest news of interest." The news Jesus came to announce is release for all prisoners of war. Those who have been taken captive by Satan have received a pardon and can be set free.

There is the story of a man who was living in sin. He

was held in prison by Satan and was unknowingly allowing himself to be kept in that prison. All he needed was enough light to show him the way out. When we share the truth of pardon and freedom already secured for us, we cause a little light to begin to penetrate the darkness. As the message of freedom began to be placed before this man, sometimes the lock would come undone, but so far the man had not realized he could go free. He still had not seen the light and was in agreement with the evil spirits who had ensnared him, so he would not leave. Satan knew if the man ever realized he could be free, there would be defeat in his camp, but Satan was confident he could keep his victim deceived and in darkness. Then a light began to shine from somewhere. There was a crack in the wall, and light was starting to shine through. It was that same light that had defeated Satan years ago. It was the same light that never condemned but illuminated Satan's evil spirits and then lit the way out of the darkness of his camp. That is where the will of the man came in. He had to choose death or life. Obviously, God had not given up on this man, but why? Why would He give him a chance when he had gone so far? Had he not gone too far to ever be useful to God? What was this light trying to do, and why had it come to this man?

Satan immediately began to try to fill in the crack and hide the light from the man, but the light was too penetrating. The crack would not be sealed. The light was shining on the man. It was letting him know he could be free. It was causing his mind to think thoughts of truth and showing up the deceitfulness of Satan and his schemes. The light was just enough to let him see the open lock. Would he push open the door and follow the light out of Satan's snare? Or would he stay where he was? Had the spirits of unbelief, fear, and indifference done their work completely, or did the man have a desire to live in the light? What would he do with the light?

This man is you and me. The question for every one of us is the same. What will we do with the light? Once we come to the light and are born again, the same question prevails: What will we do with the light we have received? Jesus said:

> Ye are the light of the world. A city that is set on an hill cannot be hid. Neither do men light a candle, and put it under a bushel, but on a candlestick; and it giveth light unto all that are in the house. Let your light so shine before men, that they may see your good works, and glorify your Father which is in heaven.
>
> —Matthew 5:14–16

As captives who have been released, we are set apart to let other captives know they can be free. Our responsibility is to give them the light. It is their responsibility to make the choice.

"[He hath sent me to preach] recovering of sight to the blind" (Luke 4:19). When something is recovered, it is regained or restored. Sight is the power to see. *Sight* also means "to discern or understand."

When Jesus died, the veil in the temple was torn in two from top to bottom. That veil was symbolic of the division between God and man due to sin. And, of course, we know that division of sin came when Adam and Eve chose to disobey God. Obviously, before that time there was free fellowship between them. Their knowledge and insight were darkened and their spiritual sight was obscured when they ate the forbidden fruit. It was as if they were looking through a veil when it came to spiritual matters.

The partition between God and man is a safeguard for man because of his sin. In the presence of a holy God, sinful man would be destroyed. When Moses came down from the mountain after being in God's presence for forty days, his face shone so with the glory of God that the people were afraid to come near him. He had to cover his face with a veil for the sake of the people, although it meant they could no longer clearly see the glory of God on Him.

In 2 Corinthians 3 Paul talks about the veil Moses had to put over his face. He said we are no longer in that era. We live in a new period of time when spiritual truth can be known by everyone, and every person who has been cleansed by the blood of Jesus can enter beyond the veil into the holy of holies—the very presence of God. He spoke of those who do not believe Jesus to be the Christ:

> But their minds were blinded: for until this day remaineth the same vail untaken away in the reading of the old testament; which vail is done

away in Christ. But even unto this day, when Moses is read, the vail is upon their heart. Nevertheless when it shall turn to the Lord, the veil shall be taken away. Now the Lord is that Spirit: and where the Spirit of the Lord is, there is liberty. But we all, with open face beholding as in a glass the glory of the Lord, are changed into the same image from glory to glory, even as by the Spirit of the Lord.

—2 CORINTHIANS 3:14–18

Jesus came to remove the veil between God and us. We can see clearly once that veil is gone. Our eyes can be enlightened to spiritual matters that were unclear before. Our sin can be obliterated and open the way for contact with the Father.

Jesus opened the eyes of many who had spiritual blindness. He also opened physical eyes. Many who had never seen before suddenly saw the face of the One who came to recover sight to the blind.

"[He hath sent me] to set at liberty them that are bruised" (Luke 4:19). Those who are crushed beneath the weight of sin and sorrow can be set free. In Ezekiel we read of strengthening the diseased and healing the sick. A disease is caused by a destructive process in a person. There is an organism there that does not belong in the body, and it causes the body to be destroyed. Isaiah prophesied that we would be healed by the stripes Jesus bore on His back.

(See Isaiah 53:5.) Physical disease can be healed through Jesus and will some day be obliterated completely.

Just as Jesus came to heal physical bodies, He also came to heal the spirits of people. Sin is a destructive disease in the lives of people. It is an organism that grows and multiplies if it is not dealt with. Jesus came to set us free from the sin nature that rules us. We do not have to be governed by sin but can be set free from sin completely through the shed blood of Jesus.

The phrase *healing the sick* means to stitch places that are rubbed and worn. It is the same process as darning socks. Usually, we just throw away a sock that has a hole rubbed in it from wear. God does not throw away people who have that problem. When we are worn and weakened through the routine of life and its hardships, we need to be stitched up and restored to wholeness. That is what Jesus came to do. That is the message people need to hear.

"[He hath sent me to] preach the acceptable year of the Lord" (Luke 4:19). This passage seems to refer to the year of Jubilee mentioned in Leviticus 25. Every fiftieth year was a jubilee year in Israel. In that year anyone who had become a slave to their countrymen would be set at liberty. Those who had sold ancestral lands because of poverty had those possessions restored to them. It is a wonderful example of our salvation through Jesus. The dispensation in which we live is one of liberty from sin and death. It is a time of restoring back to us the ground that was lost when Adam and Eve fell. The territory of spiritual sight, freedom from sin, and everlasting life can be ours. Jesus came to herald that revolutionary news.

The last indictment against the leaders in Ezekiel is this: "Neither have ye sought that which was lost" (Ezek. 34:4). Jesus is the Good Shepherd. He completed His mission on Earth and ascended to the Father, but He did not neglect the ongoing work. He passed that mantle on to those of us who have received the benefits of His message. The spiritual leaders were rebuked because they did not bring back those who were driven away. The enemies of the sheep would sometimes drive them away from the rest of the flock, and they would have to seek refuge wherever they could find it. Of course, they were no match for the enemy. Our job is to bring those who are in bondage to sin and darkness into the light.

The passage of scripture that we call the Great Commission is found in Matthew 28:18–20, and it gives us further instructions as to our mission.

> And Jesus came and spake unto them [the eleven disciples], saying, All power is given unto me in heaven and in earth. Go ye therefore, and teach all nations, baptizing them in the name of the Father, and of the Son, and of the Holy Ghost: Teaching them to observe all things whatsoever I have commanded you: and, lo, I am with you always, even unto the end of the world.

Jesus begins this command with words of encouragement. All power is given unto Him, not just in Heaven, but in Earth also. As they go about their duties at His command, they will have His empowerment. The Spirit of God will be with them to enable them to do the work.

Then, He gives them the specific duties of the job. They are to go and teach all nations, not just their neighborhoods, but all nations. Remember what Jesus told His disciples just before He ascended. He instructed them to "wait for the promise of the Father" (Acts 1:4). He told them after they received the power of the Holy Spirit, "Ye shall be witnesses unto me both in Jerusalem, and in Judaea, and in Samaria, and unto the uttermost part of the earth" (v. 8).

The word *teach* in Matthew 28 means "to make disciples." It is one thing to lead someone in the sinner's prayer and quite another to make a disciple out of him. Jesus spent three years making disciples that would be able to carry on the work once He was gone. That required teaching, living it before them, and establishing them in the principles He taught. There were times when it looked as if it was impossible, but those followers' message has gone forth and is still strong in our generation. The Holy Ghost enabled them in areas where they were weak and incapable. He does the same for Jesus' followers today.

Making a disciple is training a pupil. It takes one who has knowledge and experience and another who is willing to be instructed. These students are to be baptized "in the name of the Father, and of the Son, and of the Holy Ghost" (Matt. 28:19). They need to be identified with the Lord, because there is none other worthy to be served and worshiped. They need to publicly denounce sin and other gods and affiliate themselves with Jesus. In forsaking the world and receiving the Spirit of God within them, the sin nature is cut away even in baptism. (See Colossians 2:10–12.) It is the token of the new covenant—a cutting away of sinful nature.

These students must also be taught. Teaching happens in a variety of ways. Telling someone facts is providing them with the knowledge they need to learn something. Visual aids can help to shed light on the facts. I learn much better if someone shows me how to do something than if I have to resort to reading the directions and trying to follow them. Making disciples requires hands-on training. We must not only tell the message but live according to the example Jesus gave us. It is the job of true Christians to show new converts how to walk in the Spirit. Once we introduce them to the Savior, they need to learn to do what He did and what He told us to do.

In observing what Jesus commanded, they need to guard their thoughts, their hearts, their words, and their actions to keep from doing or becoming anything less than what Jesus has called them to do or be. The commandments of Jesus are not vague. They are very clear to anyone who wants to know them. He has a definite point for us to use as a guide for our lives. He has specific results to accomplish. Read the Gospels and pay attention to the commandments of Jesus. He speaks plainly. We are the ones who make them hard to understand, usually because we are looking for an excuse not to obey them as they are. When we look at His commands and say, "Oh, but it is too hard to lay aside my comforts and goals; surely Jesus didn't mean it quite that way," we are not observing His commandments. If we observe what He said, we will guard it as our most precious treasure. We will purpose in our hearts to keep His Word regardless of personal cost. Those are the makings of a true disciple. It is difficult to make true disciples of others without being one yourself. This is our mission; not only to do and say it, but to *be* it. This is our life's work.

Just as Jesus began the commission with words of encouragement, He ends it with the same. Not only is all power given to Him in Heaven and Earth, but He promises to be with us wherever we go. If we go to the ends of the Earth with this gospel message, He will be there with us. If we go next door with the message, He will be there, too. We are not alone. We do not go in our own power or wisdom. It is by the empowerment of the Holy Spirit that we fulfill His command—our mission.

Along with the mission of evangelizing the world, the church is a place to edify the believers. He gave apostles, prophets, evangelists, pastors, and teachers to oversee that job. They are given to the church "for the perfecting of the saints, for the work of the ministry, for the edifying of the body of Christ" (Eph. 4:12). They are responsible for completing the furnishing of God's people. Once the temple is built, it needs to be completed and furnished with holy things. True believers in Christ Jesus are saints. We have been made clean through the blood of Jesus and empowered by the Holy Spirit. We become the temple of the Holy Ghost, but we need to continue to grow and be made complete. These Christian leaders are placed in the kingdom to build up the body of Christ, not to make a name for themselves or to take a place of honor but to take on the toil of a servant of the Lord on behalf of His beloved people. It involves effort, grace, discipline, and love.

The goal for the whole of this work is singular:

> Till we all come in the unity of the faith, and of the knowledge of the Son of God, unto a perfect man, unto the measure of the stature of the fulness of Christ: That we henceforth be no more children, tossed to and fro, and carried about with every wind of doctrine, by the sleight of men, and cunning craftiness, whereby they lie in wait to deceive; But speaking the truth in love, may grow up into him in all things, which is the head, even Christ.
>
> —Ephesians 4:13–15

If every believer is guided into truth, they will have unity in their beliefs and in their work. They will not fall for the deceitfulness of the enemy. They will not be double-minded, carried away by first one doctrine and then another. They will be solidly built on the right foundation, with the right beliefs, with the right power. The point of the leadership is to train disciples of Christ in a way that will establish them in their own relationship with Christ.

Parents teach their children so eventually those children will not need the parents' training anymore. They will be mature and able to provide for themselves and their families. The same scenario applies to the role of these church leaders. They are to help mature the people of God so that they can then go out and be effective in the kingdom.

Christ loved the church—His people—enough to sacrifice His life for us. He did it to cleanse us and make us holy. Then we can be presented back to Him. (See Ephesians 5:27.) We are not asked to die for our sins or those of another, but we are asked to take the message to everyone.

THE CHURCH'S STRUCTURE

The church of Jesus Christ was created as a living entity. Remember, it is a structure made up of living stones. It is not an organization run by programs and laws of the world system. It is alive with the Spirit of God and has a platform that is on a much higher plane. Professional businesses go by a set of rules—some written, some understood. The church is called to follow the rules of the Bible—God's written, inspired Word—but it also is called to be led by and filled with the Spirit of God. The order with which the church operates should be a revelation to the world of God's kingdom. When each individual becomes one with Christ, then we are automatically one with each other. Only when we follow the leadership of the Holy Spirit can we truly be the example of Christ to the world.

As members of the body of Christ, we need one another. We need the strength and insight each member has to offer. It seems the early meetings of the church were quite different than what we are accustomed to. They had no building designated for their meetings, so they probably worshiped in homes and outdoors as necessary. Wherever we choose to worship, we are called to come together.

> And let us consider one another to provoke unto love and to good works: Not forsaking the assembling of ourselves together, as the manner of some is; but exhorting one another: and so much the more, as ye see the day approaching.
> —HEBREWS 10:24–25

> Take heed, brethren, lest there be in any of you an evil heart of unbelief, in departing from the living God. But exhort one another daily, while it is called To day: lest any of you be hardened through the deceitfulness of sin.
> —HEBREWS 3:12–13

Worship is an intrinsic part of the Christian life. It is a way to communicate intimately with our God and opens the door for His Spirit to communicate intimately with us. Worship is not our minds or emotions getting in touch with God, but goes much deeper. It is our spirit touching God's Spirit. God will come in His glory (manifest presence) to receive true worship.

Corporate worship is also imperative. It involves hearing

the Word, sharing songs, praying together, and encouraging one another. The body of Christ works together to supply everything needed for the work of God's kingdom. We all have different functions and gifts, and all are necessary. (See 1 Corinthians 12.) We need one another for strength and to bring balance. If we never fellowship with other believers, we will be unstable.

THE CHURCH'S POSITION

The church is the bride of Christ. Jesus loves the church so much that He gave His life for her.

> Husbands, love your wives, even as Christ also loved the church, and gave himself for it; that he might sanctify and cleanse it with the washing of water by the word, That he might present it to himself a glorious church, not having spot, or wrinkle, or any such thing; but that it should be holy and without blemish.
>
> —EPHESIANS 5:25–27

Jesus died to cleanse us and make us holy so He can fellowship with us on a close personal level. He is returning for His bride at an undesignated time. Revelation 19:7–8 reveals this about the Marriage Supper of the Lamb: "Let us be glad and rejoice, and give honour to him: for the marriage of the Lamb is come, and his wife hath made herself ready. And to her was granted that she should be arrayed in fine linen, clean and white: for the fine linen is the righteousness of saints." Then in

Revelation 21:2, "And I John saw the holy city, new Jerusalem, coming down from God out of heaven, prepared as a bride adorned for her husband."

If we want to be a part of the bride of Christ, we will prepare ourselves. Holiness is being separated from the world and the contamination of sin. It also involves connecting ourselves to Christ and His righteousness. If we truly want to become holy, we will separate ourselves to God and from the world. When I married my husband many years ago, I vowed to keep only to him and forsake all others. I do not flirt with other men, and I certainly do not date other men, because I belong to my husband and keep myself separate to him and from others. We must be faithful to God in that same way. To be sanctified wholly to Him is to turn away from all others and give ourselves completely to Him. Flirting with the world or dating the world is unfaithfulness and puts up a wall in the relationship. It is difficult to communicate through a wall!

Satan wants to woo us away from our loyalties to the Groom. He is sly, and we need to be aware of his devices. The Word tells us to abstain from fleshly lusts and even lists some of these things in Galatians 5:19–21. We are to keep ourselves from them. Yes, these wrong desires have declared all-out war with our spirit. But remember, we do not have to surrender to their attacks just because it is easier for the present. We have the power of the Holy Spirit to live a very different life. We must use the armor described in Ephesians 6 (truth, righteousness, peace, faith, salvation, and prayer) as well as the sword of the

Spirit, which is God's Word. It is up to us to use His weapons and armor. Jesus spoke of those who allow the cares of this world, the deceitfulness of riches, and the desires for other things to enter into their hearts and take root (Mark 4:19). When that happens, it chokes out the good seed. We lose our influence, our credibility, and our testimony in Christ. We also lose our ability to do what God has called us to.

Have you already fallen prey to the snare of the enemy? Take heart. There is a way out. You can confess to God, cry out to Him for forgiveness, and start over again. "Our soul is escaped as a bird out of the snare of the fowlers: the snare is broken, and we are escaped. Our help is in the name of the LORD, who made heaven and earth" (Ps. 124:7–8). It is God's heart to save us, not condemn us. Remember, Jesus gave Himself to cleanse us and make us holy.

God has something ahead for His bride, and now is the time to prepare. Now is the time to sacrifice our flesh for the things of God's Spirit—eternal accomplishments. We *can* be genuinely in love with Jesus and full of His Spirit within. Then our worship comes alive, and our works bear fruit. That comes from pulling ourselves away with Jesus in consistent times of personal prayer, Bible study, and worship. If nobody around you is doing it, you still can. It may set you apart as different from everyone else, but it is worth the cost.

It is time to renew our vows to God and be loyal to Him. He is looking for those who will put aside the distractions of this world and get in step with Him. It involves our interests decreasing and the interests of God becoming most important to us.

God has called a church—His bride—to work side by side with Him. Every born-again believer from every era and every place on Earth is part of His church, where He chooses to dwell.

chapter 10

Judgment

JESUS CLEARLY STATED that His mission on Earth was not to judge or condemn the world. His mission was to save the world. "For God sent not his Son into the world to condemn the world; but that the world through him might be saved" (John 3:17). "And if any man hear my words, and believe not, I judge him not: for I came not to judge the world, but to save the world" (John 12:47).

The words *condemn* and *judge* in these passages come from the same Greek word that means "to distinguish or to determine something." In this case, Jesus was clear that His first advent was to give Himself as a sacrifice and proclaim the message of salvation. It was not time for judgment, but a day of judgment will come. Jesus took on human flesh, died, and rose again to save us from condemnation when the time of judgment comes—and it *will* come for every person who has ever lived. Hebrews 9:27 tells us, "It is appointed unto men once to die, and after this the judgment."

By what standard will we be judged? We will be judged by the Word of God and our acceptance or rejection of Jesus Christ.

> He that believeth on him [Jesus] is not condemned:
> but he that believeth not is condemned already,
> because he hath not believed in the name of
> the only begotten Son of God. And this is the
> condemnation, that light is come into the world,
> and men loved darkness rather than light, because
> their deeds were evil.
>
> —JOHN 3:18–19

If a student knows they will be given a test and they want to pass it, they will listen to the teacher and study the textbook. We have the textbook (the Bible) and the Holy Spirit is our Teacher. Jesus is the Word. In order to keep from being condemned, we must believe on Him. Believing means to place our whole self on Jesus Christ for salvation and to obey His teachings. If we truly believe, we will be consistent in following Him.

In John 5:45–47, Jesus points to the Law:

> Do not think that I will accuse you to the Father:
> there is one that accuseth you, even Moses in
> whom ye trust. For had ye believed Moses, ye
> would have believed me: for he wrote of me. But
> if ye believe not his writings, how shall ye believe
> my words?

Jesus came to fulfil the Law and become the final, lasting sacrifice for our sins. God had already shown His people what was right and wrong. He gave the Law to Moses for the people. He told them the consequences if they kept it and the consequences if they rejected His Law. "I call heaven and earth to record this day against you, that I have set before you life and death, blessing and cursing: therefore choose life, that both thou and thy seed may live" (Deut. 30:19). *Choose life!* Jesus' message was the same. He set before the people by example and teachings the fulfillment of this law and urged them to choose life. He stated plainly, "I am the way, the truth, and the life: no man cometh unto the Father, but by me" (John 14:6). However, Jesus not only told us what was right and wrong, but He took all our sins on Himself and gave us His Spirit to help us change from the inside so we could do what was right. He knew we could never please God on our own. He knew we couldn't face God in judgment with sin and there was no way we could keep the Law on our own, so He took all our sin on Himself. Then He gave us a choice to accept or reject. Jesus never tried to force anyone to follow Him. He simply called them and gave them the information they needed. If they were not willing, He left them to their choice.

> He that rejecteth me, and receiveth not my words, hath one that judgeth him: the word that I have spoken, *the same shall judge him in the last day.* For I have not spoken of myself; but the Father which sent me, he gave me a commandment, what I should say, and what I should speak. And I know that his commandment is life everlasting: whatsoever I speak therefore, even as the Father said unto me, so I speak.
>
> —JOHN 12:48–50, EMPHASIS ADDED

Does a teacher fail a student? Or does the student fail himself? The teacher makes the knowledge available to succeed in their class. He can put it in the hands of the student, but cannot put it in the mind of the student. The student must make an effort to incorporate that information into his mind and life. When the examination is given on the data supplied and explained by the teacher, the student passes or fails by his own handling of the information. Our lives are like an open-book test. We have all the answers in front of us while we are taking the test. Judgment day will reveal whether we passed or failed. If we are careless and do not want to take the time to search for the answers before us, we will fail. We can take advantage of the opportunity to have the right answers and work them out in our lives, or we can reject His Word and His Spirit. Regardless of what we do, we will be judged by the Word, and our treatment of the Word of God will determine our eternal destination.

While I was studying for a Sunday school lesson, I made a list of words in the scripture passage to look up so I could have a clearer view. When I finished writing out the Greek meanings, I realized I had missed the word *Heaven*. I muttered to myself out loud, "Oh, I missed Heaven." As soon as the words were out of my mouth, a fearful sense of dread shot through me. What a terrible thing to miss Heaven! What a terrible sentence it would be to hear the Judge of all the Earth give an irreversible, eternal death sentence: "Depart from me, ye cursed [or doomed], into everlasting fire prepared for the devil and his angels" (Matt 25:41). How desperately hopeless that would be with no way to change your fate. But it does not have to be that way. Those who walk with Christ will hear, "Come, ye blessed of my Father, inherit the kingdom prepared for you from the foundation of the world" (v. 34).

Every person will one day stand before the throne of God to be judged. There are two judgments mentioned in the Bible. One is the judgment of the sinners.

> And I saw a great white throne, and him that sat on it, from whose face the earth and the heaven fled away; and there was found no place for them. And I saw the dead, small and great, stand before God; and the books were opened: and another book was opened, which is the book of life: and the dead were judged out of those things which were written in the books, according to their works. And the sea gave up the dead which were in it; and death and hell delivered up the dead which were in them: and they were judged every man according to their works. And death and hell were cast into the lake of fire. This is the second death. And whosoever was not found written in the book of life was cast in to the lake of fire.
>
> —Revelation 20:11–15

That is a sobering passage of truth from God's Word. We must be born again, or we will not be able to enter the kingdom of God in this life or the next. When one is judged by their ability to keep the Law, without the sacrifice of Jesus, they are doomed. We must accept the provision of Jesus' blood before our names will be written in the Lamb's Book of Life. This judgment is called the White Throne Judgment.

Those who are in the Book of Life will be judged for their works. There are levels of rewards for the believers. This judgment is called the judgment seat of Christ.

> Now if any man build on this foundation [the foundation of Jesus Christ] gold, silver, precious stones, wood, hay, stubble; Every man's work shall be made manifest: for the day shall declare it, because it shall be revealed by fire; and the fire shall try every man's work of what sort it is. If any man's work abide which he hath built thereupon, he shall receive a reward. If any man's work shall be burned, he shall suffer loss: but he himself shall be saved; yet so as by fire.
>
> —1 Corinthians 3:12–15

If we want our works to have everlasting effects and rewards, we must build with spiritual things from a pure heart.

"It is a fearful thing to fall into the hands of the living God" (Heb. 10:31). Jesus spoke these words in Luke 12:5: "But I will forewarn you whom ye shall fear: Fear him, which after he hath killed hath power to cast into hell;

yea, I say unto you, Fear him." Judgment is sure. None of us know when our time on this earth will end. We need to prepare now and stay ready.

Hell and Heaven

THE DIFFERENCE IS Christ whether we sing in Heaven or weep in Hell." When I was a little girl, I saw that message on a billboard along the side of the road. A sense of dread gripped my heart and sobered my mind to think of such a weighty subject. I was a Christian, so I was not afraid for me. But, I was troubled for those who made the wrong choice and had to live everlastingly in torment. What a disastrous choice of doom. Once death takes such a person out of time and places them into eternity, their fate is sealed. The other choice, of course, is to accept Jesus Christ before it is too late. Whichever choice we make for our eternal destination is made in this life. When this life ends, our destiny is sealed, whether our choice was good or bad. Judgment will not make the choice for us; it will only show which choice we have made. It will be a terrible time. I believe even the most righteous will tremble in the presence of the almighty, all holy God of the universe.

> For the time is come that judgment must begin at the house of God: and if it first begin at us, what shall the end be of them that obey not the gospel

of God? And if the righteous scarcely be saved,
where shall the ungodly and the sinner appear?

—1 Peter 4:17–18

Hell

Hell is mentioned numerous times in the Scriptures, in both Old and New Testaments. The term *Hades* is used throughout the Old Testament and means "the place or the state of those who have passed from this life." It is the region where the departed spirits of the lost abide. Before the ascension of Christ, the blessed dead were also in a section of Hades. Jesus went and preached to those souls (1 Pet. 3:18–19) and led them from captivity (Eph. 4:8–10).

Gehenna is a name for the place of everlasting punishment for those who are lost. It is described as everlasting fire prepared for the devil and his angels. "Then shall he say also unto them on the left hand, Depart from me, ye cursed, into everlasting fire, prepared for the devil and his angels" (Matt. 25:41). If you prepare a room for a guest, you get it ready ahead of time. Hell is prepared for the devil and his angels, but they will not be the only inhabitants. Satan intends to take many souls along with him, souls that could have resided in Heaven for eternity but never made the right choice.

Jesus calls these people cursed or doomed. Their time to make a decision is past and there is no other recourse now but to reap what they have sown. They are consigned to everlasting fire. During this time, they will still think, remember their life on Earth, and cry out for relief. They will even be concerned for those others who made the wrong choice, but there will be no way to change their eternal sentence. (See Luke 16:19–31.) At the end of this world "the Son of man shall send forth his angels, and they shall gather out of his kingdom all things that offend, and them which do iniquity; And shall cast them into a furnace of fire: there shall be wailing and gnashing of teeth" (Matt. 13:41–42).

Another description of the torment of Hell is outer darkness. (See Matthew 22:13, 25:30, 2 Peter 2:17, and Jude 13.) Outer darkness is outside the light. It is being on the exterior rather than inside. Jesus warned about refusing the light. He said, "And this is the condemnation, that light is come into the world, and men loved darkness rather than light, because their deeds were evil. For every one that doeth evil hateth the light, neither cometh to the light, lest his deeds should be reproved [discovered]" (John 3:19–20). If we choose to walk in darkness in this world, we choose darkness for eternity. "God is light, and in him is no darkness" (1 John 1:5). He does not even make a shadow when He turns. There is no obscurity in Him at all, but all is clear and distinct. What a horror to be banished from God's presence eternally.

I have experienced times when it *seemed* God was not there and was not listening, but I knew He was. Those times were terrible. I cannot imagine knowing I could never have fellowship with God again, that I would never again feel His Spirit leading me or convicting me. "There shall be weeping and gnashing of teeth, when ye shall see Abraham, and Isaac, and Jacob, and all the prophets, in the kingdom of God, and you yourselves thrust out" (Luke 13:28).

Just as there are degrees of rewards in Heaven, there are degrees of punishment in Hell. Luke 12:42–48 shows us this concept clearly. Verses 47 and 48 tell us, "And that servant, which knew his lord's will, and prepared not himself, neither did according to his will, shall be beaten with many stripes. But he that knew not, and did commit things worthy of stripes, shall be beaten with few stripes. For unto whomsoever much is given, of him shall be much required." Some people have sat under the anointed teaching of God's Word all their lives and still refuse to serve Him. Others may not have heard the message on a regular basis, but they have the Bible at their disposal and refuse to read it. Then others may have had none of those opportunities, yet they are without excuse, because even nature shows the glory of God (Rom. 1:20–21).

W. E. Vine's reference book, *Vine's Expository Dictionary of New Testament Words*, tells us the angels that sinned were cast into Tartarus. (See 2 Peter 2:4.) That is Hell's deepest abyss where these angels await judgment and eternal torment. These angels beheld the face of God and still rebelled against Him. Their judgment is on a severe level because of their knowledge of truth.

In Galatians 5:19–21, some of the works of the flesh are listed:

Now the works of the flesh are manifest, which are these: Adultery, fornication, uncleanness, lasciviousness, Idolatry, witchcraft, hatred, variance, emulations, wrath, strife, seditions, heresies, Envyings, murders, drunkenness, revellings, and such like: of the which I tell you before, as I have also told you in time past, that they which do such things shall not inherit the kingdom of God.

Again, in Revelation 21:8, the list of wickedness that will not be allowed in Heaven is found:

But the fearful, and unbelieving, and the abominable, and murderers, and whoremongers, and sorcerers, and idolaters, and all liars, shall have their part in the lake which burneth with fire and brimstone: which is the second death.

Wickedness cannot stand in the presence of God. That is why Jesus died—a sacrifice in our place—to free us from sin and make it possible for us to come into His presence.

"The wicked shall be turned into hell, and all the nations that forget God" (Ps. 9:17). Why go to such a terrible place of eternal darkness void of the presence of God when we don't have to? "The way of life is above to the wise, that he may depart from hell beneath" (Prov. 15:24). Obviously, we each have a choice. Listen to both choices carefully and make your decision.

Heaven

If we intend to go to Heaven when we die, we must be born into the kingdom of God in this life. "Except a man be born again, he cannot see the kingdom of God" (John 3:3). The word *see* here means "to observe, perceive, or experience." Verse 43 in Matthew 13 reads like this: "Then shall the righteous shine forth as the sun in the kingdom of their Father. Who hath ears to hear, let him hear."

Just as Hell is prepared for the devil and his angels, Heaven is prepared for the people of God. "Then shall the King say unto them on his right hand, Come, ye blessed of My Father, inherit the kingdom prepared for you from the foundation of the world" (Matt. 25:34). The children of God are those who will inherit what He has. Of course God is eternal, so when we inherit, it will not be because He is dead. We will be able to share it with Him forever.

The throne of God is there.

> And immediately I was in the spirit: and, behold, a throne was set in heaven, and one sat on the throne. And he that sat was to look upon like a jasper and a sardine stone; and there was a rainbow round about the throne, in sight like unto an emerald....And out of the throne proceeded lightnings and thundering and voices: and there were seven lamps of fire burning before the throne, which are the seven Spirits of God.
>
> —Revelation 4:2–3, 5

What an amazing picture of God on His throne! How can we even imagine what it will be like in His presence?

Who will be in Heaven? God the Father, God the Son, and God the Holy Spirit, angels, and people who have been born again. We will not have bodies as we have now, because these bodies have pain, get sick, become weary, and finally die and decay. After Jesus rose from the dead, He was able to come through closed doors. He would appear and then disappear. Yet, He could eat and drink. The disciples could see Him and touch Him. He had scars but no wounds. He was healthy three days after His crucifixion and resurrection. He had a glorified body. Ours will be glorified also. Paul tells us plainly in 1 Corinthians that we will have new bodies:

> Now this I say, brethren, that flesh and blood cannot inherit the kingdom of God; neither doth corruption inherit incorruption…For this corruptible must put on incorruption, and this mortal must put on immortality. So when this corruptible shall have put on incorruption, and this mortal shall have put on immortality, then shall be brought to pass the saying that is written, Death is swallowed up in victory.
> —1 Corinthians 15:50, 53–54

Death will be over and our spirits will be housed in new bodies that will be free from the curse that was prevalent in the Earth and in our bodies because of the sin element that entered in the Garden of Eden.

> And there shall be no more curse; but the throne
> of God and of the Lamb shall be in it; and his
> servants shall serve him: And they shall see his
> face; and his name shall be in their foreheads.
> —REVELATION 22:3–4

We will see the face of God!

Because the curse is removed, there will be no sorrow, crying, or pain.

> And God shall wipe away all tears from their eyes;
> and there shall be no more death, neither sorrow,
> nor crying, neither shall there be any more pain:
> for the former things are passed away.
> —REVELATION 21:4

This is no fairy tale. This is the reality and promise of the God who created all things and controls all things.

I have often wondered what would keep us busy in Heaven for eternity. I love to write songs about Jesus and God's Word. I love to play instruments and sing. I thought how I would miss that, and then I realized what a tremendous part music must play in Heaven. It seems we will be busy serving God in various ways. That is exciting! And there will be nothing to hinder us in any of our endeavors.

In the city of God, there will be no night, because God, who is light, will be there. "And the city had no need of the sun, neither of the moon, to shine in it: for the glory of God did lighten it, and the Lamb is the light thereof"

(Rev. 21:23). "And there shall be no night there; and they need no candle, neither light of the sun; for the Lord God giveth them light: and they shall reign for ever and ever" (Rev. 22:5).

No sin will be allowed in God's city. "And there shall in no wise enter into it any thing that defileth, neither whatsoever worketh abomination, or maketh a lie: but they which are written in the Lamb's book of life" (Rev. 21:27). Only those who have yielded to the Holy Spirit rather than the works of the flesh will be allowed to enter in. The fruit produced by these is "love, joy, peace, longsuffering, gentleness, goodness, faith, meekness, temperance" (Gal. 5:22–23).

If you look carefully, you will see that God is not interested in keeping people out of Heaven. It is His desire and His will that all will be saved, yet He cannot allow wickedness in His presence. Here again, the choice is ours.

If you travel from one country to another, they will check your luggage at the border to be sure nothing unacceptable is being brought into their country. If they find something unacceptable, you have the choice of leaving that thing behind and entering in, or keeping it and not entering in. It is the same with God's kingdom. The way has been provided for us to enter Heaven, but we will not be allowed to take any evil with us. We can choose to accept Jesus' sacrifice and leave our sin behind, or keep the sin and refuse to enter in. Therein lies our choice.

"The difference is Christ whether we sing in Heaven or weep in Hell."

Epilogue

I N THOSE DAYS there was no king in Israel, but every man did that which was right in his own eyes" (Judg. 17:6).

Our civilization has gone back in history to a time when there is no code of right or wrong. Everyone does that which is right in his own eyes. Why? What are the consequences? Where is the remedy?

"Ye shall not do after all the things that we do here this day, every man whatsoever is right in his own eyes" (Deut. 12:8). Moses spoke those words before the passage in Judges. He spoke those words when the commandments were given to them from God. It was time to lay aside their own opinions and find out what was truly right and good. God showed them plainly, yet it wasn't long before they needed a reminder again. They pushed aside His Law by reinterpreting it to suit their own notions and theories. Are we not doing the same thing today? In the end, in the judgment, God's Law will not be overridden, nor will our opinion stand as a principle of right.

Josiah became king of Judah when he was eight years old following a heritage of evil kings who sinned and caused all Judah to sin in idolatry. He, however, did what was right in the sight of the Lord, and when he was twenty-six, he gave orders to repair the temple of the Lord. As they were going through the ruins, they found the Book of the Law. When the book was read to Josiah, he became very upset.

He had not grown up knowing the Law because his father and grandfather were evil kings. (Manasseh had turned back to the Lord but was not able to reverse the evil he had done in Judah.) When he heard it he was distressed and commanded the priest and scribes:

> Go ye, inquire of the Lord for me, and for the people, and for all Judah, concerning the words of this book that is found: for great is the wrath of the Lord that is kindled against us, because our fathers have not hearkened unto the words of this book, to do according unto all that which is written concerning us.
>
> —2 Kings 22:13

To make a long story short, the prophetess of God told him God would punish his people for their sins, but it would not be in Josiah's lifetime. She sent him this word from the Lord:

> Because thine heart was tender, and thou hast humbled thyself before the Lord, when thou heardest what I spake against this place, and against the inhabitants thereof, that they should become a desolation and a curse, and hast rent thy clothes, and wept before me; I also have heard thee, saith the Lord.
>
> —2 Kings 22:19

Josiah had been ignorant of the Law, therefore he did not keep it or lead his people to keep it. Immediately after he received the Law, he began to keep it. Many people today are ignorant of the teachings found in God's Word. We will be judged by His Word. We are accountable for its message.

Now that you have been reminded, what will you do with the information? We can learn the order of God, but then we must begin to allow it to work out in our lives. "Wherefore, my beloved, as ye have always obeyed, not as in my presence only, but now much more in my absence, work out your own salvation with fear and trembling" (Phil. 2:12). We are not to "make up" our own salvation but take the truth of God's Word and put it into action in our everyday lives. We are to do this with fear and trembling, not with flippancy. We are to recognize the power and awesomeness of the God who *is*.

> Take heed, brethren, lest there be in any of you an evil heart of unbelief, in departing from the living God. But exhort one another daily, while it is called To day; lest any of you be hardened through the deceitfulness of sin. For we are made partakers of Christ, if we hold the beginning of our confidence stedfast unto the end; While it is said, To day if ye will hear his voice, harden not your hearts, as in the provocation.
>
> —HEBREWS 3:12–15

To Contact the Author

www.counterfloministries.com

Patti Hedgepath Lusk
P. O. Box 736
Belton, SC 29627

counterfloministries@hotmail.com